PLANT

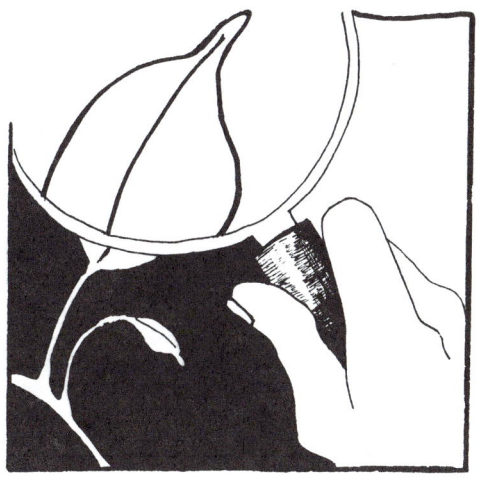

BASICS

A MANUAL FOR THE CARE OF INDOOR PLANTS

By Susan McCollum
and Teena Risley

This book is available through
Garden Tapestry, Inc.
Publishers of Tropical Plant Technician
719 W. McGraw, Seattle, WA 98119
Telephone (206) 213-0162   Fax (206) 270-9146

Copyright ©1994 by

McCollum, Risley & Associates
9809 Ceralene Drive, Fairfax, VA 22032

Price: $14.95
Fourth Printing

All rights reserved. No part of this book may be reproduced in any form or by any means without permission in writing from the publisher.

Design Consultant: Ralph N. Ives

Cover and Text Illustrations:
Patricia Chapman Meder

Plant Care Guide Illustrations:
Plantscape, Inc. © 1992

Composition: Wordworks

Printing: Colortone Press

ISBN 0-9644264-0-4

Table of Contents

Introduction, v

BASICS OF PLANT CARE
The Plant, 3-5
Watering Plants, 7-9
Grooming Plants, 11-12
Pruning and Pinching, 13-15
Maintaining Flowering Plants, 17

MANAGING PLANT HEALTH
The Foliage Environment, 21-23
The Root Environment, 25-29
Insects and Mites, 31-35
Infectious Diseases, 37-41
Environmental Diseases, 43-44
Troubleshooting, 45-47
Integrated Pest Management, 49-51

PLANT CARE GUIDE, 53-82

Glossary, 83-84

Index, 85-86

Introduction

WELCOME to the world of interior landscaping where nature comes indoors. In our world of indoor gardening, offices, hotels, restaurants, shopping malls and homes come alive when tropical and flowering plants are added to interior spaces.

Although indoor gardening actually got its start in Europe in the 1800's, it wasn't until the 1970's that plants were no longer considered a luxury. Today, plants fill both functional and aesthetic needs. As a design element, plants act as a living art form, providing a welcome contrast to the concrete and steel buildings that we work in. Graceful palms and delicate ferns soften the harsh angular lines of our furnishings. Broad-leafed *Dracaenas* and exotic *marginatas* make a bold statement in monochromatic spaces. Majestic *Ficus benjamina* specimens add interest to lobbies and other expansive interiors.

Recent studies indicate that people are unhappy in the absence of greenery. Psychologists call green the color of peace and serenity; yet, our climate controlled living and working spaces isolate us from nature. Tropical and flowering plants put nature back into our homes and offices. Employers who invest in greenery say there are positive changes in their employees' morale, creativity and productivity when plants are added to work areas. Doctors and nurses report that their patients get well faster when they are surrounded with greenery or have a window with a scenic view. Hotels with atriums find that guests ask for the rooms that overlook the lush tropical forest. It is evident that plants provide an important psychological function by fulfilling our desire to live in harmony with nature.

In a two-year study that concluded in 1989, an environmental scientist, Dr. Bill Wolverton, and a National Aeronautics and Space Administration research team, found that plants reduce many of the harmful toxins found indoors. According to the scientists, common indoor plants absorb pollutants through their leaves, roots and the bacteria that live on them and convert these substances to food. Since indoor air pollution poses a major health threat, the findings present a significant discovery that may help us solve the problem called "sick building syndrome."

Our need to bring nature indoors has defined the industry we call interiorscaping. Our trademark is lush tropical and colorful flowering plants in indoor settings. Our job is to keep plants healthy so they maintain their beauty for many years.

BASICS OF PLANT CARE

NOTES

The Plant

THE "SCIENCE" OF CARING for indoor plants begins with an understanding of the basic physiological functions of plants. This foundation of knowledge serves as a starting point for learning what plants need to stay healthy indoors.

Parts of a Plant

There are four main parts to a plant: the **roots, stem, leaves** and **flowers**. The **roots** anchor the plant in the potting media and absorb water and nutrients through tiny root hairs at the tip of each root. Roots help purify the atmosphere by filtering toxic air through the soil. Roots exchange gases during the respiration process and store excess carbohydrates (plant food) for future use.

The **stem** supports the plant, stores excess carbohydrates and transports water, growth hormones, minerals and carbohydrates throughout the plant. The leaves attach to the stem at a point called the node. Axillary buds (latent dormant buds) are located at each node. The space between each node is called the internode.

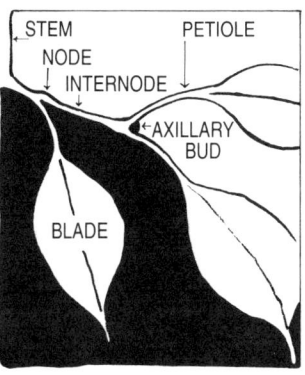

The **leaf** is composed of the blade (leaf surface) and the petiole (leaf stem). Sessile leaves are an exception. In the sessile leaf, the blade is attached directly to the stem; the petiole is missing (i.e. *Dracaena deremensis* 'Janet Craig'). Leaves produce food for the plant during the process of photosynthesis. Specialized openings called stomates in the leaves exchange gases and cool the leaf surface by transpiring water vapor.

Leaves are classified as either simple or compound. Simple leaves are composed of a single blade. The blade of a compound leaf is composed of multiple leaflets.

The **flowers** are the plant's sexual reproductive organs. Flowering is controlled by the duration, quality and intensity of available light. Generally, tropical foliage plants do not live in indoor conditions that promote flowering. Flowers that do form are usually small and insignificant and are pulled off, with a few exceptions, as they are produced.

 DID YOU KNOW ...

Not all roots are alike. Plants that prefer low light conditions have thick, fleshy roots that store water. High light plants have dense fibrous root systems that absorb water quickly.

Basic Plant Functions

Photosynthesis

In the presence of sunlight, plants convert carbon dioxide (CO2), water and minerals into plant food in the form of carbohydrates. The plant takes in carbon dioxide through the stomata, the microscopic openings on the underside of the leaves. The roots absorb water and minerals from the soil. The chlorophyll (green coloring) in the leaves converts the sun's radiant energy into the chemical energy of food. Oxygen is a by-product of photosynthesis and is given off into the atmosphere.

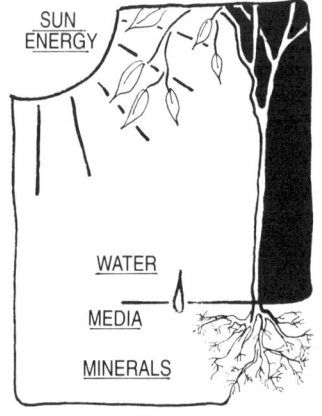

Respiration

Respiration is the opposite process of photosynthesis. During respiration, a plant takes in water from the roots and oxygen from the stomata or roots and breaks down the stored carbohydrate which releases energy. Plants use this energy to function and grow. Carbon dioxide is a by-product of respiration and is given off into the atmosphere by either the stomata or the roots.

 **DID YOU KNOW...**

Roots help purify air during the respiration process. As water drains from growing media, air is pulled into the empty pore spaces. Roots use the oxygen during respiration. Bacteria in the media help filter organic pollutants out of the air.

Translocation

Translocation is the movement of water and minerals through the plant. Plants keep cells turgid (firm) and distribute water, minerals and carbohydrates by means of translocation. Food and auxins (growth hormones) are transported downward from the foliage through vascular cell tissue called phloem. Water and minerals are transported up from the roots through vascular cells called xylem. Damage to stem tissue can disrupt translocation and weaken or kill the plant.

Transpiration

Plants cool their leaf surfaces and maintain humidity levels around the foliage with water that evaporates through the stomata. This process is called transpiration. The rate at which a plant transpires depends on environmental factors such as humidity levels and temperature. High temperatures and low humidity levels cause a plant to transpire rapidly in order to cool the leaf surfaces. If a plant transpires faster than it can draw water up, the stomata close to conserve the remaining water and the plant wilts. High temperatures and high humidity cause

✔ **TIP: First Aid For Wilted Plants**
Changing the environmental conditions that caused the plant to wilt or produce excess moisture will allow the stomata to reopen and help the plant return to normal transpiration rates. For example, if a wilted plant is sitting in a sunny window, move it to a cooler location until it recovers.

roots to continuously pump water up the stem and force droplets out openings in the leaves. These droplets, called 'water of guttation' contain minerals. When the water evaporates, the remaining minerals (salts) burn leaf tips and margins.

Acclimatization

Acclimatization is the process by which a plant adapts to a new environment. A plant's growth habits, water and nutrient usage, physical appearance and cell structure change with new environmental conditions.

In their native environment, most tropical plants thrive in high light intensities, warm even temperatures and high humidity levels. The indoor environment is very different. It is characterized by low light levels, dry air and temperature fluctuations.

A plant grown in high light, high humidity conditions has smaller, thicker, lighter colored leaves with shortened internodes. In some plants, the leaves will be oriented vertically or will be cup shaped. Roots are extensive and the foliage variegation is bright and colorful. Under these conditions, the plant uses water and nutrients rapidly and grows quickly. Excess food is produced and stored for future use.

A plant placed indoors needs to adapt to lower light and dryer air than it received in its growing environment. A plant may need from 1 to 10 weeks to adjust to its new location, depending on the species, its overall health and the acclimation treatment the plant received prior to placement. As the plant adapts to the indoors, it sheds excess foliage it can no longer support. Newly formed leaves are flatter, thinner, more supple and are oriented horizontally. Low light plants have greener leaves due to increased chlorophyll levels which amplify the plant's ability to produce food.

In lower light, the plant begins to slow its metabolism down. Less food is produced and water and nutrient requirements decrease. Roots become thicker and produce fewer root hairs.

✔ **TIP: Acclimating Plants**
Help your plant adjust to the indoor environment by:

- *Gradually reducing the amount of water supplied*
- *Removing excess fertilizer*
- *Pruning out inner leaves and overlapping foliage*
- *Keeping the plant clean and pest free*

NOTES

Watering Plants

ALMOST 90% of a plant's internal makeup is water. Plants use water to produce food through photosynthesis, transport nutrients and hormones, cool foliage and maintain the firmness (turgidity) of leaves and flowers.

Plants have varying water needs. High light plants need more water than plants with medium and low light requirements. Plants that need high light usually have dense, fibrous roots systems that dry out quickly and require more water than the lower light plants. Plants that tolerate lower light have fewer, thicker roots that store water and do not need to be watered as often.

The key to proper watering is to maintain a correct balance of water and air-filled pore spaces in the growing medium. This is achieved by watering a plant thoroughly, then allowing it to "dry down" as much as possible without stressing the plant or allowing it to wilt.

When to Water

Plants start to show subtle signs of water stress, such as dull-looking foliage and a slight droop to the leaves, when they need water. Learn what a plant looks like when it is healthy and not in need of water. It will make it easier to notice subtle signs of water stress at other times.

Another method of deciding when a plant needs re-watering is to feel the growing media and lift the grow pot to feel the weight of the moisture content. With experience, your sense of touch will guide you in watering plants. A "moderately moist" growing media feels cool or barely moist to the touch. When you press it between your fingers, it holds together. When the moisture drops below "moderately moist," it is usually time to re-water the plant. When using the "feel" method, be aware that cold or sandy media may seem wet when it is actually dry. Double check the moisture content by lifting the grow pot. Dry media is light and wet media is heavy.

The amount of moisture in the media will vary from the top to the bottom of the pot and from side to side. Therefore, it is important to feel a sampling of soil throughout the container. Use a soil probe to reach to the bottom of the pot. Pull the sample out and feel the moisture at different depths. If the soil stays in the probe, it is moist; if it falls out of the probe, it is dry. If the media at the bottom of the pot is still wet, you may have to wait a week or more before watering this plant.

 DID YOU KNOW...

The re-watering point is different for each plant species, the health of the plant, the growing medium, the size of the container, the environmental conditions and the time of year. Be aware of any changing environmental or health related conditions that effect the plant's water usage.

8 / BASICS OF PLANT CARE

 TIP: Is It Time To Water?

Review these steps when deciding to top water your plant:

- *Observe plant for subtle signs of water stress.*
- *Feel growing media for moistness.*
- *Lift container for weight of media.*
- *Take a core sample for accurate measurement of moisture.*

Top Watering

When the media dries sufficiently, water the plant thoroughly to make sure the entire medium is moistened. Pour enough water into the container so that a little water trickles out the holes in the bottom of the grow pot. Remove excess water standing in the container. This method of watering is called leach irrigation. Soluble salts are flushed out of the media and stale gases are pushed out of the pore spaces and exchanged for fresh gases.

Subirrigation

Subirrigation systems, commonly referred to as self-watering containers, regulate the amount of water a plant receives and take away the guesswork involved in top watering. Plants on subirrigation generally do not need to be watered as frequently as top-watered plants. For this reason, subirrigation can save time, especially when caring for many plants.

There are a number of subirrigation systems on the market. All systems operate on the same principle: water is added to a reservoir at the base of the container and pulled upward through the growing media to the roots by capillary action. Water soluble fertilizers can be added to subirrigation water, although the recommended application rate should be reduced.

Plants Under Water Stress

Overwatering problems

Plants that receive too much water become stressed and eventually die if the condition is not corrected. When the air-filled pore spaces in the media are filled with water, the roots cannot exchange gases between the atmosphere and the roots. The saturated soil smothers the roots and they begin to die. As the root hairs wither, they stop absorbing water and the plant wilts. This condition makes the plant vulner-

 TIP: Drying Out Saturated Media

Try these ideas to dry out an overwatered plant:

- *Refrain from adding additional water.*
- *Remove top dressing until media is dried out sufficiently.*
- *Temporarily remove plant to warmer, higher light area.*
- *Repot plant into fresh media.*
- *Stick strips of capillary matting into top few inches of media; capillary matting will help wick moisture from soil.*
- *Remove plugs of saturated media from direct planted plants; add fresh plugs of media.*

able to diseases such as stem and root rots. Secondary infections such as molds and fungi may grow on rotted tissue. Finally, the stressed and weakened plant is unable to function normally.

The symptoms of overwatering are general and non-specific. Noticing signs of stress in the plant and closely monitoring the plant's water absorption will help you quickly diagnose overwatering problems.

Underwatering Problems

Underwatered plants are generally easier to diagnose than overwatered plants. Plants wilt due to lack of turgidity in the foliage and stems. The root ball becomes dry and compacted. The plant may lean out of the pot and drop brown or yellow leaves.

Plants will not recover from a wilt caused by underwatering if allowed to reach a point where the vascular cells collapse. This point is called the Permanent Wilting Point (PWP). A plant cannot be saved from a wilted condition if the petioles collapse and bend over the rim of the pot, the roots are dry and brittle, and over 40% of the foliage reaches the PWP.

✔ **TIP: Reviving a Wilted Plant**

Follow these steps to revive a wilted plant:

- *Water growing media in stages to allow the media to absorb the water.*
- *If root ball has contracted and pulled away from the sides, add 1 Tbls dish soap to 1 gal water to break up adhesion.*
- *Use warm, not tepid water.*
- *Break up compacted media with fingers; fill in sides with fresh media.*
- *If possible, move plant to cooler, humid conditions.*
- *Prop up or sleeve wilted foliage to speed recovery.*
- *Remove yellow foliage and leaves with bent petioles to help plant recover quickly.*
- *Prop up or repot leaning plants; support plant until roots develop.*

NOTES

Grooming Plants

Groom plants to keep them healthy, clean and attractive. Grooming involves cleaning the foliage, removing debris and trimming or pulling off dead leaves and stems.

Cleaning plants

Dust or dirt build-up on leaves interferes with various plant functions. A regular cleaning keeps plants healthy and alerts you to any signs of pest infestation or environmental stresses.

Plants coming directly from the grower may have whitish residue on the leaves. To remove it, use a commercial leaf cleaner, a weak solution of oxalic acid and water, or gently rub the leaves with a DRY cloth or towel.

To clean a build up of dust on foliage, wash the leaves with 1 tsp non-phosphate dish soap in 1 qt water. Use a sponge, cleaning cloth or paper towel to wipe the leaves clean.

Be sure to wash both sides of the leaf. Clean plants with hairy leaves (cilia) with a brush or duster.

Feather dusters may be used to clean the foliage of large plants with lots of small leaves. **WARNING!** Dusters can easily spread mites and insects, so keep your duster clean. Wash the duster regularly with insecticidal soap and water or spray it with an alcohol and water solution. Store the duster in a paper bag combined with an insect pest strip when you are not using it.

✔ **TIP: Cleaning The Tough Stuff**

A build up of grime, dirt or insect residues can be removed from foliage with glass-cleaning products (that do not contain ammonia), or a bio-degradable cleaning product that does not contain phosphate (check the label). Mix 2-8 Tbls/gal of water. Spray the solution on the plant until it runs off the foliage or use a dampened sponge or cleaning cloth to wipe grime off the leaves. Do not scour leaf surface harshly as it may damage the leaf cuticle. Add ½ tsp of insecticidal soap to aid in the cleaning process. Test for phytotoxic reactions (evidence of damage such as leaf burning or yellowing) on a single leaf before applying to the rest of the plant.

Removing debris

Debris found on the plant, on the top of the soil or at the bottom of the container should be cleaned out regularly. The plant will look more attractive and there will be no place for insects or disease to develop. Dead leaves, trash thrown on the top of the soil and debris fallen into the bottom of the container harbors insect or disease. Wash both the outside and inside of the decorative container to remove dirt, grime and any pest infestations that may be present.

Trimming

Keep the plant attractive by trimming off old flower heads and blemished leaves. Leaves with blotches and brown or yellow tips should be removed entirely. Discolored tips on leaves are symptomatic of a plant problem. It is better to solve the problem that caused the leaf tipping in the first place rather than treat the symptoms.

If you do decide to trim or pull the brown tip off the leaf, leave a small margin of yellow or brown; do not cut into the healthy tissue. Continuously trimming off unsightly tips repeatedly wounds the living plant tissue and prevents it from callusing or scabbing over. The leaf will continue to turn brown and decline. If you leave a callused margin, it may stop the browning from continuing up the entire leaf. Always keep scissors sharp and clean the blade with alcohol.

 TIP: Plant Grooming List

Plants are well-groomed when they are:

- *Free of dust, dirt and grime.*
- *Have no debris in the container or on top of the soil.*
- *Have no yellow, brown, blemished leaves or flowers.*

Pruning and Pinching

PLANTS LAST LONGER and keep an attractive shape when they are routinely pruned and pinched. Both procedures are necessary to maintain the plant's natural beauty and to keep the plant free of dead and decaying stems, leaves and branches.

As a plant ages, it changes shape as it responds to the light in its environment. For example, plants stretch towards the light source. If they are not rotated, they become thick and bushy on one side and thin and leggy on the other side. Or, if a high light plant, such as a *Ficus benjamina,* is placed in low light, it drops leaves in the center of the plant to allow the available light to filter through. As the plant changes shape, help it maintain a balanced appearance. Achieve this by rotating the plant, if possible, and by pinching and pruning it to promote new growth and to control its height and width.

Pinching

Pinching is a technique that involves removing the growing stem tip (apex) of the plant. This stops the flow of auxins (growth hormones) which regulates bud dormancy and allows the dormant buds found on the stems to develop into branches and leaves. Pinching works well on new plants such as *Aglaonemas,* crotons, aralia, pothos, nepthytis and ivies.

Pruning

Pruning is a technique that involves removing plant stems or

✔ TIP: Pinching Keeps Plants Bushy

Pinching is done with the forefinger and thumb, or with a small pair of scissors or clippers. Pinch off the growing tip slightly above a node. Be careful not to harm the lower leaves or buds. Axillary buds on the lower leaves will now develop into stems and branches.

branches to force new growth. Prune to refoliate and shape an older plant, to control the shape and fullness of a younger plant, or as a cultural control to remove insect or disease infected plant parts. Although pruning may be done at any time during the year, the plant will respond more quickly to the cuts at the beginning of the plant's active growth period, usually around early spring.

The first step in pruning any plant is to decide on the overall shape you want the plant to

NOTES

have. Remember, interior plants should be natural looking rather than tightly pruned. To open the plant up and give it a graceful look, remove side branches. To keep it compact and bushy, cut the main stem.

Always use sharp, clean scissors or pruners. Make the cut above a node on the limb to be removed. When pruning branches, be careful not to cut into the branch bark collar. This swelling at the base of the branch contains natural antibodies that help ward off disease. Always make complete cuts; never rip or tear a branch as this will leave the plant vulnerable to infection.

When you routinely groom your plants and carefully time pinching and pruning to promote new growth, your plants will retain their shape, fullness and health.

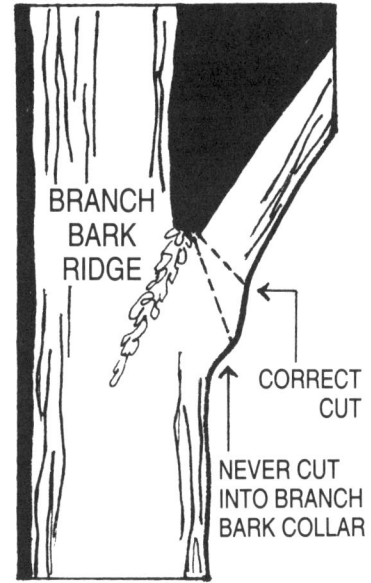

 TIP: Pruning to Force New Growth

Selectively cut branches to force new growth in the direction you want the plant to grow. Remember to cut further back on the stem to allow the new growth to fill in naturally.

Vary the heights of the cuts made on branches to avoid an unnatural shape.

NOTES

Maintaining Flowering Plants

FLOWERING PLANTS are an important color element in the indoor foliage display. They do not represent the same long-term investment as tropical plants; yet, they are a significant cost and must be maintained correctly to get full value from the investment.

The life span of a flowering plant depends on the amount of light and water the plant receives. Most flowering plants prefer bright filtered light and evenly moist soil. Most varieties do not like to dry down between waterings. For this reason, flowering plants may need to be watered twice a week. Placing the plant on subirrigation will extend the time between watering.

Most flowering plants should be installed in the early stages of blooming when they are just beginning to show color. The flowers will open over a period of time, extending the enjoyment of the plant. Poinsettias and hydrangeas are two exceptions; if not already in full bloom, they will not peak in an indoor setting. Discard the plant when the leaves yellow and drop or when the flowering cycle is over.

Handle flowering plants with care. In cold climates, they must be protected with paper or fiber sleeves and transported in heated vehicles. In warm climates, they should be transported in air-conditioned vehicles. Do not keep plants sleeved for more than 12 hours. Remove plant sleeves carefully. Blossoms and stems are delicate and break easily.

✔ **TIP: Caring For Flowering Plants**

Extend the life of flowering plants by:

- *Maintaining correct moisture levels*
- *Picking off spent blooms*
- *Pruning out broken branches and yellowing foliage*
- *Rotating plant weekly to evenly distribute light*

NOTES

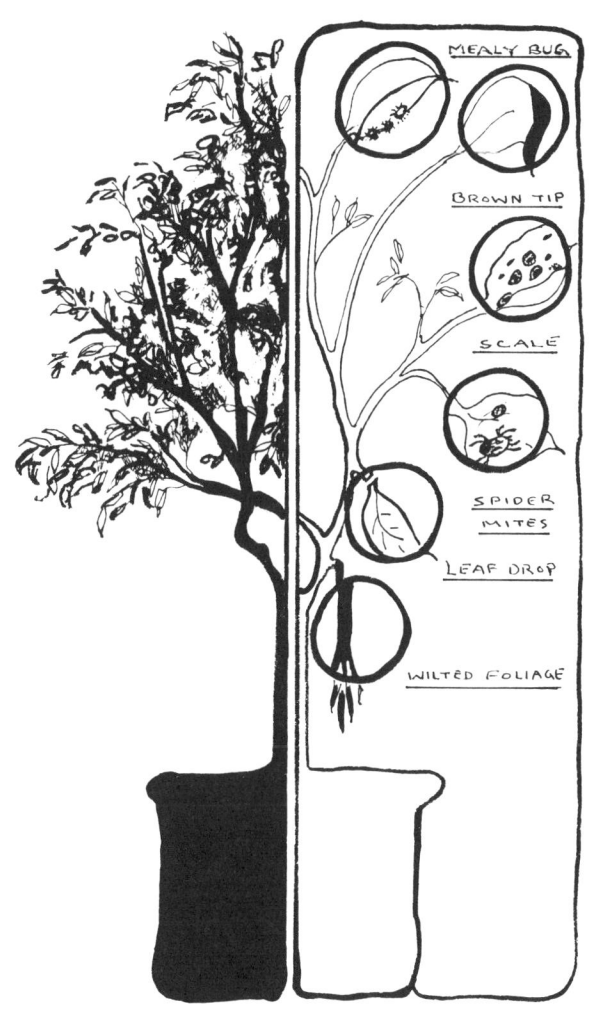

MANAGING PLANT HEALTH

NOTES

The Foliage Environment

LIGHT, TEMPERATURE, relative humidity and air quality are environmental conditions above the soil line that influence a plant's health.

Light

Indoors, the amount of light a plant receives is a compromise between the needs of the plant and the needs of the humans who live and work in the same space. Yet light is critical to a plant's health. Without an adequate supply of light, photosynthesis and other plant functions do not take place. The plant, weakened by inadequate light, is susceptible to health problems.

Plants vary in the amount of light they need to survive. In general, the more light a plant receives, the faster it grows and the more water and nutrients it uses. Plants that tolerate low light levels grow more slowly and need less water and fewer nutrients.

Light has three elements: intensity, duration and quality. Each element has a direct relationship to the overall health of the plant. Understanding the properties of light and its role in plant health will help you keep plants healthy.

ments for plants range from 10 footcandles (fc) to over 500 fc. The average light intensity indoors is 50 - 500 fc.

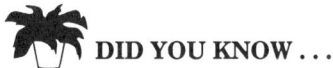 **DID YOU KNOW . . .**

The amount of light a plant receives is not constant. Light intensity varies with the changing of the seasons, differing window treatments and shading from objects found both indoors and out. This varying amount of light intensity will affect your plant's water usage and growth habits.

Light Intensity

Light intensity refers to the brightness of light. Light intensity is measured in footcandles. A footcandle is the amount of light that one "international candle" will emit over one square of surface area when the candle is one foot away. Light require-

Light Duration

Light duration refers to the total number of hours of light a plant receives in a day. The day length (photoperiod) regulates photosynthesis, flower production and other plant functions. Photoperiods of 8-16 hours are best for indoor plants.

Light Quality

Light quality refers to the different wave lengths or colors that make up visible (white) light. Although sunlight appears to be white, it is really a blend of many colors: red, orange, yellow, green, blue and violet rays. Plants respond best to the red and blue wavelengths in visible light. Unfortunately for the plants, the artificial lights we have in our homes and offices usually do not emit strong blue and red wavelengths. This is because human skin tones appear healthier in light that emits yellow, orange wavelengths and pale or sickly in light that emits blue and red.

Cool white fluorescent bulbs balance the needs of people and plants and are currently the best compromise bulb available. Whenever possible, plants should receive some natural sunlight for optimal plant health.

✔ **TIP: Living with Available Light**

Help your plants thrive in existing light conditions by:

- *Being aware of the optimum light requirements for the plant.*
- *Providing correct moisture levels for plants in varying light conditions.*
- *Watching for changes in light intensity or duration that will have an adverse effect on the plant.*
- *Rotating plants to evenly distribute light on foliage.*
- *Pruning to maintain fullness in uneven light situations.*

Temperature

The optimum temperature range for indoor plants is 55-85F. Most indoor environments fall between 60-80F; it is common to find temperatures fluctuating above or below that range within the same building.

Temperature changes create health management problems that start with plant stress and may lead to pest infestations and diseases. For example, low temperatures retard plant growth. Leaves may develop spots and curl downward. Roots and stems may develop infectious rots. On the other hand, high temperatures may cause wilting and utilization of stored food reserves. Leaves may develop brown or yellow tips and necrotic (dead) spots. Plants subjected to high temperatures are susceptible to insect and mite problems.

Relative Humidity

Relative humidity refers to the amount of moisture held in the air. Although most tropical plants prefer a relative humidity (RH) level above 80%, the indoor environment is closer to 20% RH. Low humidity levels cause wilting, decreased food production, browning or necrosis (dead tissue) of the leaf margins, small, brittle leaves and plants with dull-looking foliage. Although rare indoors, high humidity levels may cause molds and mildews to develop. Temperature and humidity levels affect most pests directly. Spider mites survive best in warm, dry conditions. Infectious rots and mildews flourish when plants are subjected to humid, cool conditions.

✔ **TIP: Stabilizing Humidity Levels**

The following suggestions may help to stabilize humidity levels:
- Water plants properly.
- Move plants away from drafts or vents.
- Place plants on a tray of wet gravel.
- Group plants together.

Air Quality

The quality of the air around the plant's foliage is important. Plants need carbon dioxide and oxygen for photosynthesis and respiration. Both are normally found in generous amounts indoors. Imbalances may occur in areas where there is little air movement such as conference rooms or other areas not used daily. Plants placed in these spaces may produce small, malformed foliage and experience slow growth.

Plants can filter some organic pollutants from the atmosphere. The leaves absorb and oxidize the pollutants during the process of photosynthesis and respiration. Bacteria in the growing medium filter organic pollutants out of air used by the roots.

NOTES

The Root Environment

CONDITIONS BELOW the soil line are critical to the plant's health. Two factors affect the root system: 1) the physical make-up of the root environment, and 2) the nutritional make-up of the root environment.

The Physical Make-up of the Root Environment

The growing media provides moisture, support, minerals and good aeration to the roots. The medium should be porous and well drained, yet have the ability to retain enough water for the plant's needs. The growing media should have the correct amounts of nutrients available for the plant, be low in soluble salts and have pH between 5.5 and 7.0. It should be slow to decompose and free of diseases, weeds and harmful chemicals.

Growing media

The growing media is composed of media particles, water and pore spaces. Most of the media used with tropical plants is "soilless media." This sterilized material consists of organic matter mixed with course textured inorganic amendments such as perlite (expanded volcanic ore), vermiculite (expanded mica-like mineral), styrofoam pellets, sand, volcanic rock and calcined clay. The organic material in soilless media may be sphagnum peat moss, tree bark, rice or peanut hulls or sawdust.

DID YOU KNOW . . .
Growing media changes as it ages. Newly installed media may shrink or shift in the container. Older media compacts as organic materials decompose. Soil pH changes as soluble salts build up in the media. Be aware of these changes by monitoring your growing media regularly.

Pore spaces

Pore spaces are important in the growing medium. Roots exchange gases as they metabolize their food. Compacted or water-saturated media can starve the roots of the air they need and eventually kill the plant. When watering a plant, the pore spaces fill with water. As the water drains out due to gravity, evaporation and root absorption, the spaces fill with air. A good growing media provides a balance between water-filled and air-filled pore spaces.

Media Water

Water regulates the soil temperature and carries dissolved nutrients up through the plant. Water also moves gases through the medium. When water is added to the soil, it pushes stale gases out of the pores. As the water drains out of the medium, it pulls fresh air into the empty pore spaces.

NOTES

The Nutritional Make-up of the Root Environment

Plants are unique because they make their own food (carbohydrates). The materials they use to make this food come from the nutrients found in air, water and the growing media.

 TIP: Your Plant's Food Production

Help your plants produce food by:
* *Cleaning foliage with phosphate-free soap and water.*
* *Providing proper maintenance to keep plants healthy.*
* *Rotating plants located in uneven light sources.*
* *Pruning plants for optimum light exposure to all leaves.*
* *Monitoring nutrient levels in the growing media.*

The essential elements

There are 16 nutrients that plants need for normal growth. Carbon, hydrogen and oxygen are supplied by water and air. The growing medium supplies the remaining elements. Nitrogen, phosphorus, potassium, calcium, magnesium and sulfur are called major, or macro nutrients, because the plant uses these elements in large amounts. The remaining elements are called micro, or trace elements, and are needed in small amounts. The trace elements are iron, zinc, boron, copper, manganese, molybdenum, and chlorine. A complete fertilizer will have a mixture of both the major and minor nutrients.

Fertilizers are actually salts and should be used carefully to avoid burning the plant's root system. Water soluble fertilizers are powders, liquids or granules that are dissolved in the irrigation water and applied directly to the media or poured into the subirrigation system. These fertilizers are preferred because it is easy to control the nutrient levels in the potting medium. Should a toxicity problem arise, the water soluble fertilizer can be easily leached from the media.

 DID YOU KNOW ...

Fertilizer nutrients bond to soil particles in the growing media. Positively charged nutrients, or cations, are attracted by negatively charged anions in the media. The cation exchange capacity (CEC) of a medium refers to the ability of a growing media to hold and store nutrients. Some media amendments such as vermiculite and peat moss have high CEC and will hold nutrients in the medium. Sand and perlite have low CEC and do not hold fertilizer salts as well.

When to fertilize

Plants should be fertilized during the time of active growth. Although this varies from plant to plant, most plants slow down their growth during the winter months. As spring approaches and temperatures and daylength increases, the plants begin to "flush out" with new growth and vigor. Fertilizing should coincide with this activity.

Plants with high light requirements use more water, produce

more food and generally grow at a faster rate than plants in lower light conditions. Consequently, high light plants deplete the nutrient levels in the media faster than low light plants and need to be fertilized more often.

✔ **TIP: When NOT to Fertilize**

Not all plants need to be fertilized regularly. Do not fertilize plants in the following situations:

- *Plants that are stressed or sick. Plants need to be healthy to use the nutrients. Stressed plants grow slowly and may be damaged by excess fertilizer.*

- *New plants arrive with plenty of food reserves. Do not add any fertilizers for 6-12 months.*

- *Wilted plants. The high concentration of salts in the dry medium will burn plant roots.*

- *Plants with timed release fertilizers in the medium. Growers sometimes add these before shipping. Adding more fertilizer will burn roots and the plant will decline.*

Managing fertility problems

It is important to carefully plan a fertilizing program for your plants. Improper fertilization practices can cause numerous problems for plants grown indoors. Nutrient deficiencies may be caused by lack of a specific nutrient or by the plant's inability to intake nutrients due to root damage or excess soluble salts.

Plants exhibit specific characteristic symptoms for each nutrient deficiency. Nitrogen, phosphorus, magnesium, potassium, and zinc all have symptoms that show up on the older or lower leaves first. Calcium, boron, manganese, sulfur and iron symptoms show up on newer or bud leaves. Take note of both general and specific symptoms when diagnosing a deficiency problem.

Over fertilization of indoor plants is common. The resulting concentrations of soluble salts damage the roots, foliage and weaken or kill the plant. Monitor the nutrient levels in the growing media by periodically testing for changing pH and soluble salt build up.

Soluble salts

A build up of salt in the growing media may be caused by excessive fertilization or by using water containing salts (sodium chloride, calcium carbonate, iron sulfates, etc.). Excessive soluble salts cause many plant problems including root burn and leaf necrosis or blotching. A white crust of salt may build up on the rim or drainage holes of the container.

pH levels

pH is the measure of relative acidity of the growing medium. Most media used with tropical plants have a pH of 5.5 - 7.0 (pH above 7 are basic; below 7 are acidic). A change in the pH may cause nutritional imbalances and affect the absorption of water by the roots. Soluble salt build up and decomposing organic matter increase the acidity of the container media. Adding dolamitic lime or calcium nitrate will raise the pH; adding iron sulfate or ammonium sulfate lowers the pH.

 TIP: Controlling Soluble Salts

Control the level of soluble salts in growing media by:
- *Regularly monitoring soluble salt levels.*
- *Removing excess fertilizer pellets from top of media.*
- *Removing excess water from saucers; dissolved salts leached out during watering may re-enter media if not removed.*
- *Periodically replacing top few inches of subirrigation media where soluble salts have built up.*
- *Tracking fertilizer schedules to avoid over-fertilizing.*
- *Routinely leaching growing media of top watered plants.*
- *Repotting with fresh media.*
- *Removing soil plugs of growing media from direct planted plants and filling plugs with fresh media.*

NOTES

Insects and Mites

THERE ARE relatively few serious pests of indoor ornamental plants; however, they can do significant damage if undetected. To diagnose and treat pest problems, learn to identify the pests that attack tropical and flowering plants, recognize the symptoms of a pest infestation and know what to do if an outbreak occurs.

Aphids

Appearance

Soft-bodied, pear-shaped insects with "tail-pipe" like processes called cornicles extending from the rear of their bodies. They may be either winged or wingless. Aphids are usually less than 1/8" long and come in shades of green, brown and red. They cluster in large colonies on new growth, stems, buds and on the under surface of leaves.

Life Cycle

When actively feeding, aphids give birth to live young, almost identical in appearance to the adult, and undergo a gradual metamorphosis. New generations are produced every 14 days in temperatures above 60F.

Damage

Aphids damage plants by sucking plant sap through their specialized mouth parts. Aphid infestations reduce plant vigor, and curl and distort leaves. Sticky residue (honeydew) on the plant reduces photosynthesis and promotes the growth of sooty mold. Aphids may also transmit viral diseases when feeding.

Control

Cultural/Mechanical — Wash off sooty mold and honeydew. Prune out heavily infested areas. Avoid high levels of nitrogen in the media.

Chemical — Spray weekly with 1 tsp phosphate free soap in 1 gal water directly on the insects. Remove aphids with rubbing alcohol on a cotton swab. Use an interiorscape/indoor approved pesticide such as insecticidal soap or horticultural oil.

Fungus Gnats

Appearance

Dark-colored, delicate flies, less than 1/8" long.

Life Cycle

Adult females can lay up to 300 eggs in 10-day period in the growing media. Eggs hatch in about 6 days, producing white maggots with dark heads. Larvae grow to 1/4" within 2 weeks, then form pupae. Adults emerge from media in less than a week.

Damage

Adult fungus gnats do not damage the plant; small clouds of flies appear when the infested plant is disturbed. The larvae stage of the fungus gnat damages plants by feeding on organic matter (including roots) in the growing media. Diseases may enter damaged plant tissue. Symptoms of infestation are overall decline in the plant's appearance, stunting, yellowing and defoliation. Growing media may be saturated and smell bad.

Control

Cultural/Mechanical — The presence of fungus gnats usually indicates the media is wet and organic matter is decaying. Allow media to dry out. Remove top dressing and siphon off standing water. Move the plant to brighter light. Do not crowd plants. Remove fallen debris from soil surface. Replace top 4" of soil with fresh sterilized soil. Wash pot saucers to kill maggots.

Chemical — Apply soil drench using an interiorscape/indoor approved pesticide such as insecticidal soap or a microbial insecticide. Trap adults with sticky monitoring cards.

Mealybugs

Appearance

Six-legged insect with a flattened oval body. A white waxy secretion covers the insect and projects a distinctive fringe around its body.

Life Cycle

Eggs are laid in a compact, cottony, waxy sac at axils of branching stems or leaves. Eggs hatch in about 10 days into crawlers; crawlers wander about, feeding on plant before reaching maturity in 6-8 weeks. The crawler stage is most vulnerable as it does not have the waxy sac that protects the adults and eggs.

Damage

Citrus and long-tailed mealybugs pierce the stems and leaves and feed on the sap. Root mealybugs attack roots in the media. The plant may be damaged further by disease which enters through the wounds. Mealybugs excrete honeydew. The sticky, sweet substance provides growing conditions for black sooty mold. Honeydew and mold reduce the amount of light absorbed by the leaves during photosynthesis.

Control

Cultural/Mechanical — Prune out infested branches. Wash off honeydew and sooty mold. Remove infested top dressing. Clean grow pot and container with soap and water. Avoid high levels of nitrogen in the media.

Chemical — Spray a mixture of rubbing alcohol and water directly onto the insects or, dab the insect with a cotton swab dipped in alcohol. Use an interiorscape/indoor approved insecticidal soap or horticultural oil. Follow label directions for repeated applications.

Scale

Scales are piercing-sucking feeders, related to mealybugs. Most adult females have no legs; they feed during the immature stages of their life cycle. The winged males have legs, but no mouth parts and do not feed. Scale insects may go unnoticed until the host plant is extensively damaged. They look like natural bumps or blisters on stems and branches.

There are many types of scale found on indoor plants. They can be categorized in two groups: soft scales and armored scales.

Appearance

Soft Scale: The covering of the adult female is flattened, soft and pliable, shiny, yellowish-brown with dark brown grid-like mottling. The insect remains attached to its shell when the scale is lifted off plant tissue. It is typically found along leaf veins and stems. Brown soft scale, hemispherical scale and black scale are classified as soft scales.

Armored Scale: Armored scale covering comes in a variety of textures and colors depending on the species. Armored scale produces little honeydew in comparison to the soft scale. The body of the female is formed of wax and cast off skins of earlier molts. Typically found on stems, branches and leaves, the armoured scale remains attached to the host when the shell is picked off. Common armored scale found on indoor plants include Boisduval's scale, California red scale, Florida red scale, fern scale and cactus scale.

Life Cycle

Females reproduce by either laying eggs or giving birth to live young. During the crawler stage, the insect is very active and may travel some distance over the plant until it settles down. Once the crawler inserts its stylet (mouthpart) into the host plant, it remains immobile for the rest of its life. Scales normally require 4 weeks to 6 months to complete development. In a protected environment, there may be 3-6 generations a year.

Damage

Scale insects damage plants by sucking sap from tender growing parts of the plant, reducing plant vigor and appearance.

Some species excrete a sweetish honeydew which gives rise to development of black, sooty mold and weakens the plant.

Control

Cultural — Prune off infested branches before crawlers hatch. Mist or hose plant to remove honeydew and dislodge crawlers. Increase amount of light plant receives. Reduce levels of nitrogen in growing media.

Chemical — Wipe off individual scale with rubbing alcohol on a cotton swab. Treat plants with an interiorscape/indoor approved insecticidal soap, horticultural oil or foliar spray according to label directions. Remove sooty mold with alcohol or 1 tsp vinegar in 1 gal water. Follow with soap and water spray.

Spider Mites, two spotted and red

Appearance

Mites are not insects; they are 8-legged and closely related to spiders. Less than 1/50", oval bodies, yellow-green with two dark spots, or reddish in color. Bristles on humped back.

Life Cycle

Females lay approximately 200 eggs that hatch into 6-legged larvae. Larvae stage is followed by 8-legged nymph and adult stages. The spider mite life cycle (from egg to reproducing adult) varies with temperature; 7-10 days at 80F and 20 days at 70F.

NOTES

Damage

Gray or yellow stippling of upper leaf surfaces produces a mottled appearance. In severe cases, webs form on leaves and stems; leaves may dry and fall.

Control

Cultural/Mechanical — Remove all forms of plant stress. This includes removing the plant from hot, dry areas, filtering sunlight with curtains or blinds and lowering fertilizer rates. When possible, isolate plants.

Chemical — Spray at 7-10 day intervals with an interiorscape/ indoor approved insecticidal soap, miticide or horticultural oil. Follow label instructions. To prevent future infestations, provide correct environmental conditions and wash foliage with 1 tsp phosphate free soap in 1 gal water on a regular basis.

Thrips

Appearance

Tiny winged insects 1/5" in size, usually tan, black or yellow.

Life Cycle

Life cycle takes 2-5 weeks, depending on the weather. Adults lay eggs in plant tissue. Eggs hatch quickly in warm weather and wingless nymphs feed on plant sap. Thrips pupate in the growing media and adults fly up to feed and lay eggs in the plant.

Damage

Thrips scrape plant tissue and suck sap from the wound. Diseases may develop on damaged tissue. Thrips can be found on foliage and flowers of plants. They exude black spots of fecal matter.

Control

Cultural/mechanical: Spray forcefully with soap and water. Increase humidity levels.

Chemical: Use an interiorscape/ indoor approved pesticide such as insecticidal soap or horticultural oil. Trap adults with sticky monitoring cards.

Whitefly

Appearance

Tiny winged insects about 1/16" in size. Adults are covered with a powdery wax. Nymphs resemble mealybug and scale.

Life cycle

Adults lay eggs in a circle on underside of leaves, which hatch in 7-10 days. Nymphs are active for several days until they molt and become immobile. For the next 7-14 days, the pupae go through several stages and produce the characteristic whitish wax. Winged adults emerge and repeat the cycle. The entire life cycle takes 18-25 days depending on the temperature.

Damage

Whiteflies suck plant sap and produce honeydew which attracts sooty mold. Damage includes wilting, yellowing, loss of vigor.

Control

Cultural/mechanical: Vacuum off winged adults with hand vacuum; trap adults with yellow sticky monitoring cards.

Chemical: Use an interiorscape/ indoor approved pesticide such as insecticidal soap or horticultural oil.

NOTES

Infectious Diseases

A CONTROLLED ENVIRONMENT and proper maintenance generally keep plants healthy and vigorous. When infectious diseases do develop, three conditions are always present.

(1) There is a disease pathogen, a living agent such as fungi, bacteria, or viruses.
(2) The host plant is genetically susceptible to the pathogen.
(3) Environmental conditions weaken the plant and contribute to disease development.

To control an infectious disease, you must eliminate one of the three conditions required for disease development.

Fungi

Fungi are minute organisms, lacking chlorophyll. They grow as fine thread-like filaments in circular, overlapping lesions. Often there are concentric rings in the lesions which give a bull's eye appearance.

Most fungi produce a multitude of spores which function similarly to seeds. Each spore can start a new infection. Fluffy, moldy growth on the surface of the plant and black, pinpoint-like pustules within a lesion indicate a fungal disease is present.

Some of the more common fungal diseases found in the interiorscape include leaf spots, stem and root rots, powdery mildew and blight.

Leaf spots

Appearance
Symptoms include spots of various sizes, shapes and colors, "shot-holes" in leaves, yellowed and withered foliage and overall poor plant health. Leaf spots generally have a dry appearance.

Control
Cultural/Mechanical — Fungal disease can be spread by air, water, insects, or people. Take care when handling infected plants. Avoid splashing water on leaves, disinfect tools and equipment, destroy

---

✔ **TIP: Prevent Diseases On Your Plants**

Prevention is the preferred method of disease control. Pathogens do not have the opportunity to get established when you incorporate these practices into your plant care program.

- *Use healthy, disease-free plants.*
- *Use sterilized potting media.*
- *Don't crowd plants; allow air to circulate freely around plants.*
- *Water plants without splashing leaves.*
- *Routinely disinfect tools and hands with alcohol or bleach.*
- *Control insect and mite populations.*
- *Remove and destroy infected plants, media and top dressing.*
- *Maintain appropriate environmental conditions.*
- *Remove standing water from bottom of containers.*

NOTES

infected staging. Trim out and destroy infected portions of the plant.
Chemical — Use fungicide labeled for interiorscape/indoor use.

✔ TIP: Disease-Free Tools

Stop the spread of diseases by sterilizing your maintenance tools. Using a cotton swab, wipe 70% rubbing alcohol on scissors, pruners, soil probes, tips of watering cans and the ends of watering wands. Rinse sponges, cleaning cloths and dusters in a mild solution (1/8 cup to 1 gal water) of sodium hypochlorite (Clorox), then wash with soap and water. Sterilize decorative containers with a solution of 1/4 cup sodium hypochlorite in 1 gal water.

Stem and Root Rots

Appearance

Roots become soft, mushy, collapsed or hollow. They appear dark brown or black and few or no white roots or root tips are found when the root ball is washed free of soil. Root tissue may slough off leaving a whitish string of core tissue. Stems die back from terminal tips to main trunk; foliage withers and falls off. Margins of leaves die.

Control

Cultural/Mechanical — Remove top dressing. Avoid excessive soil wetness. Keep soil from becoming compacted. Avoid contaminating other plants by sterilizing tools. Repot in fresh media.

Chemical — An indoor/interiorscape-approved soil drench fungicide is sometimes effective to combat root rot.

Powdery Mildew

Appearance

Powdery white growth appears on leaves, flowers and stems. Powdery mildew usually will not kill a plant; however, unsightly fungus lesions reduce the quality of the plant.

Control

Cultural/Mechanical — Water early in the day to allow humidity levels to drop by afternoon. Increase air circulation, but avoid cold drafts. Do not crowd plants together. Trim off and destroy infected plant parts.

Chemical — Spray baking soda mixture (1 Tbls baking soda, 2 Tbls insecticidal soap or horticulture spray oil and 1 gal water) on mildew. An approved soil drench fungicide is sometimes effective.

Blight

Appearance

Dark spots on stems, leaves or flowers; rotted or malformed flower heads; water-soaked lesions on infected plant parts; dieback of tissue. Obvious signs of infection such as cottony masses of mycelium may appear on soil surface or gummy exude and pink masses of spores appear at bases of infected stems.

Control

Cultural — Keep foliage dry, reduce humidity levels at night and avoid crowding plants. Increase air circula-

tion. Cut off and destroy infected plant parts. Sterilize tools.
Chemical — Use appropriate fungicide as required.

Bacteria

Plant diseases caused by bacteria are less common than fungal diseases. When they do occur, they are potentially damaging since bacterial infections spread quickly and most are systemic.

Bacterial pathogens are single-celled, non-spore forming, microscopic organisms. Bacteria usually enter the host plant through a wound or natural opening.

Bacterial infections thrive in moist, humid conditions. When the disease is present, pests or people who touch the plant may transport the bacteria to wet leaf surfaces. Water splashing from contaminated soil onto plant parts may also spread the infection. Sound cultural practices, like those listed above, are the preferred way to inhibit the introduction or spread of this pathogen.

Bacteria often appear as oily, greasy or water-soaked spots on leaves. Other symptoms include stem or leaf rots, sour smelling stems or roots, cankers and wilting. One common sign of many bacterial diseases is the foul-smelling, slimy-brown ooze coming from infected tissues.

Bacterial leaf spots and stem rots

Appearance

Leaf spots are dark green, greasy, water-soaked areas, sometimes surrounded by a yellow halo. A slice of the lesion placed in a drop of water emits a brownish ooze of bacteria. Stem rots are mushy and foul-smelling. Bark sloughs off in your hand when you touch the plant.

Control

Cultural/Mechanical — Promptly remove and destroy infected plant or plant parts. Disinfect all tools that come into contact with a bacterial infection. Avoid splashing water from contaminated soil onto plants.
Chemical — Use a bactericide control registered for interiorscape/indoor use.

Viruses

Viruses are microscopic pathogens, consisting of a single strand of DNA and a protein coating. Viruses cannot penetrate an intact host. They enter a plant through an opening caused by injury, pruning or grafting, by insect feeding activity or by worker's hands or tools. Currently, there are no chemical controls for viruses.

Appearance

Symptoms of viral infections are diverse and can easily be mistaken for other causes. The most common clue to viral infection is the sudden onset of symptoms. Some of the symptoms associated with viruses are: stunted growth; mosaic pattern on leaves; distorted leaves and leaf tips; yellow streaking of leaves; yellow ring spots or lines on leaves; cup-shaped leaves; uniform yellowing, bronzing or reddening of leaves; crinkling or curling leaf margins.

When a viral disease is suspected, isolate the diseased plant and obtain a diagnosis from a plant disease clinic.

Control

Cultural — Use only virus free plants. Destroy virus infected plants, disinfect tools, avoid wounding plants and control or eliminate insects that spread disease.

Chemical — None currently available.

✔ TIP: Are You A "Vector?"

Stop the spread of infectious diseases by following these sanitary measures:

- *Sterilize tools including soil probes, pruners and sponges.*

- *Wash hands after treating a diseased plant or touching the growing media.*

- *Be aware that spores or infected plant tissue clinging to clothing and hair may be carried to healthy plants.*

- *Do not re-use infected growing media or decorative containers unless sterilized.*

- *Control pest infestations on infected plants. Pests transmit diseases when they pierce plant tissue during feeding.*

NOTES

Environmental Diseases

ENVIRONMENTAL, OR ABIOTIC DISEASES, are caused by noninfectious disease conditions, such as low light, high soluble salts or temperature extremes. Abiotic diseases do not grow, reproduce or spread from plant to plant. They weaken a plant and allow secondary infections and infestations to develop.

The key to diagnosing abiotic problems is to recognize both general and specific symptoms on the affected plant. A general symptom is one that points to many different problems, any one of which might be the real cause of the plant's decline. A specific symptom helps you eliminate some of the possibilities by leading you to the most probable cause of plant distress. For example, brown leaf tips are general symptoms for low humidity, pesticide injury, fertilizer toxicity, overwatering and underwatering and a host of other possibilities. But, brown leaf tips in combination with the specific symptoms of yellow blotching on leaves and a whitish crust on the holes at the base of the growing container may lead you to suspect soluble salt damage, an abiotic disease.

Diagnosing problems

Abiotic diseases generally occur because of poor maintenance practices (i.e. overwatering, underwatering, dirty plants), mechanical damage (i.e. ripped or torn branches), environmental extremes (i.e. low humidity, cold or hot temperatures), pesticide phytotoxicity (i.e. incorrect application or dosage) or poor quality growing media (i.e. nutrient deficiencies, high soluble salts). The symptoms of these problems are diverse and include leaf yellowing and necrosis, water-soaked spots, distorted growth, wilting or foliage drop. Diagnosing an abiotic disease is difficult as many of the symptoms resemble those of infectious (biotic) diseases.

The chart on page 44 will help you begin diagnosing abiotic diseases. Notice that the general symptoms for each of the problems are the same; the specific symptoms help to isolate a single cause.

Controlling abiotic diseases

The most effective method of controlling or eradicating environmental disease is to change the conditions that caused the disease to develop. For example, if overwatering is the problem, cut back on water and watch plant closely to see if new growth is affected. Treat secondary infections or infestations that occurred when the plant was in a stressed condition.

✔ **TIP: Healing Your Plant**
Bring your plant back to glowing health by practicing proper maintenance procedures. A plant weakened by environmental diseases may be slow to recover, so water carefully and do not fertilize. Keep the plant clean and debris-free. Watch the new growth for signs of recovery or re-injury. Remove damaged foliage and stems. Repot plant if growing media is the culprit.

Diagnosing Abiotic Diseases

General Symptom	Specific Symptom	Problem
Leaf tipping Foliage wilt Stunted growth	Compacted, dry media Canes/stems leaning Roots burnt, brittle Leaves drop yellow/brown Brown leaf tips Entire leaf bright yellow	Underwatering
Leaf tipping Foliage wilt Stunted growth	Root/stem rot Media wet/stagnant water New growth pale/small Drops green leaves Yellowing leaf tips	Overwatering
Leaf tipping Foliage wilt Stunted growth	White crust on pot/soil Yellow blotches on leaves Burnt/brittle roots Tipped/stunted new growth Brown/scorched leaf tips	Soluble salt damage
Leaf tipping Foliage wilt Stunted new growth	Brown leaf tips/edges Dull foliage Brittle leaves	Low humidity
Leaf tipping Stunted growth	Yellow/brown/black spots Brown tips/margin on leaf Distorted/abnormal growth Film/residue on foliage Ring spots/crinkling leaf	Pesticide injury

Troubleshooting

LEARN TO DETECT plant problems before they reach crisis proportions. Your ability to recognize symptoms and diagnose the cause of the problem is critical to the health of your plants.

Diagnosing plant problems is often challenging. A plant's poor health may be due to more than one factor. For example, an environmental condition, like extreme heat, may weaken a plant and make it vulnerable to a secondary problem such as spider mites. Although the spider mites produced the visible symptoms, the hot, dry environment was equally responsible for the plant's decline.

Even when symptoms are obvious, the diagnosis can still be confusing. Insects, diseases and poor maintenance often produce the same general symptoms. Leaf yellowing and browning of the tips or edges may be due to poor watering practices, soluble salt build-up in the media, nutrient deficiency or a host of other problems. The first step in improving the plant's health is to correctly diagnose which problem is creating the symptoms.

Learning to Diagnose Plant Problems

With training and experience, you will become skillful at detecting and solving plant problems. The following three-step process will help you get started as a diagnostician.

(1) Know what a healthy plant looks like. Only by recognizing the color and vigor of a healthy plant can you begin to pick up on the subtle signs that indicate the plant is declining.

(2) Understand potential problem situations that can contribute to plant stress. A stressed plant is more susceptible to insect and disease than a healthy plant. Poor maintenance and unsuitable environmental conditions are the most frequent reasons for plant stress. Over- or underwatering, low light, extreme hot or cold temperatures and low humidity are additional factors that weaken plants. You stand a greater chance of keeping plants healthy if you select a plant that is suitable for the environment, maintain it according to its needs and know what insects or diseases it is prone to.

(3) Look at plants in a methodical, orderly manner. Start by checking the overall health of the plant, then take a close-up view.

The overall perspective. As you approach the plant, focus on its overall health. Ask yourself the following questions: *Is the plant turgid or limp? Are canes leaning? Is it dropping any leaves? Are they yellow or green? Is the leaf color good or is there evidence of yellowing? What is the plant's environment? Is it sitting in the hot sun? drafty doorway? dark hall?*

NOTES

Close-up view. As you clean and water the plant, look closely at the health of the leaves and stems. Use a hand lens magnifier (10x lens) to inspect questionable areas more closely. Look for: *necrotic (dead) area; honeydew (sticky coating); white, cottony masses; leaf spots; webbing; bumps or blisters; black mold; die back; mushy canes.*

Use a soil probe to check the moisture level in the media. Smell the sampling to detect a sour odor. If you question the health of the roots, pull the plant out of its container or try to grab a sample of the roots with the soil probe.

Keep a record of the symptoms you observe. If you're not sure what you're dealing with, ask for help or continue observing the plant for one more week. Sometimes early symptoms do not pinpoint the cause of the problem. For example, leaf spots are a general symptom that may be due to overwatering, pesticide spray, nutrient deficiencies or diseases. Plants with general symptoms may need to be watched for several weeks to see if secondary symptoms develop. Oftentimes the secondary clues are more conclusive than the primary ones when trying to isolate the problem.

The overall perspective and the close-up view should be a routine part of your regular plant care program. This is the best way to spot a problem and correct it before it does further damage.

✔ TIP: Become a Plant Detective

Acquire skill in troubleshooting plant problems by:
- *Being aware of what a healthy plant looks like.*
- *Learning the symptoms of poor plant health.*
- *Recognizing potential problems.*
- *Developing your powers of observation.*

NOTES

Integrated Pest Management

INTEGRATED PEST MANAGEMENT (IPM) is a method of pest control and eradication that combines cultural, mechanical, biological and chemical controls.

An integrated approach to pest management begins with healthy, pest-free plant material and focuses on keeping the plant healthy by placing it in the correct environment, practicing correct maintenance procedures and closely monitoring the plant for pest problems. When problems do occur, the IPM approach aims at restoring the plant to health by selecting the least toxic control strategies before relying on heavy-duty pesticides.

Cultural Controls

Cultural or mechanical controls refer to techniques used to change the plant's physical environment, the condition of the host plant or the behavior of the pest in order to prevent or suppress the pest.

Common cultural practices include aerating the soil, pruning diseased limbs, removing soluble salts, increasing humidity levels and changing watering or fertilization regimes. Other practices consist of isolating infected or infested plants, washing plants with soap, hand picking bugs, disinfecting tools and equipment and using sticky yellow cards to capture and monitor flying insects.

When establishing cultural practices, it is important to address environmental stresses that weaken the plant. Physiological disorders such as imbalances in light, temperature, moisture and soil create conditions that make the plant susceptible to pathogens, insects and diseases. Cultural practices to modify the environment include protecting plants from the hot sun or blasts of air from heating or air conditioning vents; stabilizing temperatures by making seasonal adjustments; improving or maintaining the health of the plant with proper fertilizations, pH adjustment and moisture control.

Biological control

Biological control is a pest control strategy that calls for using a living organism to control another less desirable living organism. The biological control agents (beneficials) are insect or mite predators or parasites.

On existing indoor plantings, the switch from chemical to biological controls takes careful planning and timing. Before introducing beneficials, toxic chemicals must not be present on the plants. It may take a month or more for the long-term effects of residual pesticides to wear off. During this time, pests can be kept in check with soap sprays, cultural controls and a few mild pesticides. When used as directed, insecticidal soaps, horticultural oils and Bacillus thuringiensis dusts are safe to use with biological control organisms.

Regular plant inspection and monitoring go hand in hand with the use of biological controls. Once the beneficials are introduced in the environment, you must inspect and monitor both the pest and the beneficial population to verify that the beneficials are feeding. If the pest population exceeds the tolerable level, the beneficials must be reintroduced to the environment. The success of the program is measured by the rate of decline of the pest population.

✔ TIP: Using Beneficial Organisms

To use beneficial organisms effectively, consider the following factors:

- *Beneficials are selective; no one beneficial will control all pests.*
- *Identify the pest to be controlled and correctly match the beneficial organism to the target pest.*
- *Beneficials are effective as long as there is food (target pests) available.*
- *Beneficials need to be applied to plants with each new infestation.*
- *Beneficials can be killed by accidental pesticide spraying.*
- *Use pesticides that will not harm beneficial organisms. Be aware of the plants that have biologicals on them.*
- *Beneficials are a living perishable product and must be purchased and used in a timely fashion.*
- *Keep records on your biological control program including beneficials used, successes and failures, and pesticide applications.*

Chemical controls

Chemical controls rely on pesticides and least toxic chemicals, such as rubbing alcohol and phosphate-free dish detergent, to control infectious pests and microbes. In some instances, chemicals may be the best solution to a pest problem; in other cases, you may only want to use them when other options of pest control have failed.

If chemical control is necessary, there are usually many options available to you. Products vary in a number of ways including efficacy, persistence, mobility, toxicity and mode of action. For example, insecticidal soap, a contact pesticide, must touch the pest to be effective. *Oxamyl 10G*, a systemic pesticide must be absorbed by the plant and transported to the site of activity where it is ingested by the insect.

When choosing a pesticide, read the label carefully. The label will tell you whether the pesticide is registered for use indoors and what pests the manufacturer claims the product will control. The label also lists plants that will not be harmed by application of the pesticide. Try to select a product that does not have an offensive odor or leave visible powdery residues on the foliage.

Be aware that you are required by law to follow all the directions on the label. Read it carefully. The label will tell you how to protect yourself and the environment when using the pesticide, and how to mix, spray, dispose and store the pesticide. Never ignore label warnings!

As a general rule, wear goggles, rubber gloves and boots,

inhaler and a pesticide resistant suit when handling restricted-use pesticides. Cover floors, rugs and surrounding areas with drop cloths or plastic sheets. Never mix or dispose of pesticides in sinks or areas where people mix and prepare food. Wipe up any spilled or dripped pesticide immediately and dispose of clean-up materials according to pesticide label directions. Wash hands thoroughly after applying a pesticide. Keep the pesticide concentrate in the original labeled container at all times.

Under Federal law, only certified applicators may use restricted-use pesticides. Restricted-use pesticides are those classified by the Environmental Protection Agency (EPA) as harmful to humans, animals or the environment. When a pesticide is classified as restricted, the label states **"Restricted Use Pesticide"** in a box at the top of the front panel. Pesticides that are unclassified have no designation on the product label. Contact your state extension office for complete information about pesticide use and the legal requirements in your area.

✔ **TIP: The Keys To Integrated Pest Management**

Keep your plants healthy in the interiorscape by following these IPM procedures:

- *Choose healthy, acclimated, pest-free plant material.*
- *Provide the proper environment for the plant species.*
- *Use horticulturally correct maintenance procedures.*
- *Monitor plants closely for signs of infestation.*
- *Treat infestations with a combination of cultural, mechanical, biological and least toxic chemical solutions.*

NOTES

PLANT CARE GUIDE

Aglaonema species

COMMON NAME: Aglaos; chinese evergreen. Varieties include: 'Silver Queen'; 'Maria'; 'Emerald Beauty'; 'Romano'

FORM: Bush/clump form (2'- 4')

LIGHT RANGE: Low to medium light (50fc - 250fc)

©1992

WATER REQUIREMENTS: In low light (35fc - 100fc), allow media to dry down 1/2 of container; in medium light, 1/3 of container. Water new plants around base of stems; water older plants evenly over entire surface. Use tepid water to avoid cold damage to roots and foliage.

WATER STRESS SYMPTOMS: Overwatering symptoms include mushy, yellowing leaf tips; stem and root rot; pale new growth. Underwatering will show up as brown leaf tips, older foliage turning bright yellow, leaves droopy and dull, stems leaning out of container.

MAINTENANCE TIPS: *Aglaonemas* will rot easily, so avoid overwatering. Cold temperatures and drafts will retard growth, cause blotching and leaf necrosis, and root or stem rot. Remove flowers to conserve food reserves. Prune leggy stems 1/2" above soil (or above stem node) to refoliate.

PEST & DISEASE PROBLEMS: Mealy bugs, aphids, scale, spider mites, stem and root rots, blight diseases.

Beaucarnea recurvata

COMMON NAME: Pony tail palm, elephant foot palm, bottle palm

FORM: Upright tree form with curving, ribbon-like leaves arising from central stem apex

LIGHT RANGE: Bright indirect light to direct sun (250+fc)

WATER REQUIREMENTS: Water entire root ball thoroughly. Bulb-like trunk stores water, so allow media to dry down 1/2 to 3/4 of container before watering again.

WATER STRESS SYMPTOMS: Underwatering symptoms include brown foliage, dessicated roots and shriveled stem. Overwatering symptoms include yellowish foliage, pale new growth and stem and root rot.

MAINTENANCE TIPS: Pull off brown foliage. *B. recurvata* tolerates temperature extremes and direct sun. Keep plant in container only slightly larger than trunk to avoid overwatering stress.

PEST & DISEASE PROBLEMS: Spider mites, mealy bug, scale, crown and root rot.

©1992

Brassaia actinophylla

COMMON NAME: *Schefflera,* Hawaiian *Schefflera,* umbrella tree. Varieties include 'Amate'

FORM: Bush

LIGHT RANGE: Low to medium light (50fc - 250fc)

WATER REQUIREMENTS: In low light (50fc - 150fc), water around base of stems, then allow media to dry down to 1/2 of the pot. In medium light, thoroughly water entire root ball, then allow media to dry down to 1/3 of container.

WATER STRESS SYMPTOMS: Overwatering symptoms start on older foliage. The older leaves turn yellow and fall off. Eventually all the leaves turn yellow, droop and fall off. Stems turn black and fall over with rot. Underwatering symptoms include mottled yellowish foliage that droops against stems. New growth is pale and limp. Stems lean out of pot.

MAINTENANCE TIPS: Hand wash or spray foliage to clean plant. Petioles of Schefflers are brittle and can be damaged easily. Lower foliage and suckering growth will die back in low light. Refoliate thinning plants by selectively cutting back stems to promote bushy growth. *Brassaia* species are sensitive to excessive fluoride and soluble salts and will display mottled foliage and necrotic edges from this condition.

PEST & DISEASE PROBLEMS: Spider mites, scale, mealy bug, nematodes, thrips, leaf spot, stem and root rot.

Brassaia actinophylla

RELATED SPECIES: *Schefflera arboricola.* *Schefflera arboricola* has smaller leaves and a more extensive root system than *Brassaia actinophylla.* In bright, indirect light (250+fc), the *arboricola* needs a lot of water. If overwatered, the plant sheds green leaves.

Schefflera arboricola

Cactaceae family

SPECIES NAME: *Cereus peruvianus; Cereus monstrosus; Euphorbia acurensis*

COMMON NAME: Cactus

FORM: Branching; columnar

LIGHT RANGE: Medium to high light (150fc - 250+fc)

WATER REQUIREMENTS: Water around base of plant and let media dry sufficiently. In low light (under 100fc), allow media to dry out completely. In higher light, media should dry down 3/4 of pot. Before adding water, check the stems and blades; leaf blades should feel soft and spongy to the touch.

WATER STRESS SYMPTOMS: Overwatering symptoms include yellowing leaf blades; stem and root rots. Stems become mushy, smelly and fall over. Underwatering symptoms include withered stems and foliage and necrotic rots. Entire plant may lean and fall out of container.

MAINTENANCE TIPS: Cacti store large amounts of water and can go for long periods of time in between watering. Allow plant to dry out before adding additional water to avoid root and stem rots.

PEST & DISEASE PROBLEMS: Scale, stem and root rots.

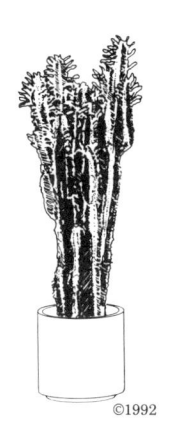

©1992

Caryota mitis

COMMON NAME: Fishtail palm

FORM: Upright slender palm with arching compound fronds. Pinnules (leaflets) have ragged edge and "fishtail" shape

LIGHT RANGE: Medium to bright indirect light (80fc - 250+fc)

WATER REQUIREMENTS: Water entire root ball thoroughly. In medium light, allow container to dry down 1/3 to 1/2 of container; in higher light, 3" to 1/4 of container, depending on light intensity.

WATER STRESS SYMPTOMS: Underwatering symptoms start with brown edges on fronds, progressing to entire frond turning brown and collapsing. Unopened stalks develop brown tips. Overwatering symptoms develop yellowish blotchy edges with discoloration progressing up entire frond. Roots develop rot.

MAINTENANCE TIPS: Prune off older discolored foliage. Wash foliage regularly to keep healthy and pest free. Fronds develop brown edges due to low humidity or water stress and yellowish edges due to low light. Yellowing fronds may be caused by iron deficiency. Water with tepid water to avoid root damage with cold water.

PEST & DISEASE PROBLEMS: Spider mites, scale, stem and root rot.

©1992

Chamaedorea species

COMMON NAME: Bamboo palm *(C. erumpens);* reed palm *(C. seifrizii);* parlor palm *(C. elegans)*

FORM: Upright clump form. *C. erumpens* and *seifrizii* may reach 14'; *C. elegans* only 6'

LIGHT RANGE: Low to medium light (50fc - 250fc)

WATER REQUIREMENTS: In low light (under 100fc), allow media to dry down 1/2 of the container; in medium light, 1/3 of the container. Pour water evenly around entire container to reach the extensive root system of the *Chamaedoreas.*

WATER STRESS SYMPTOMS: Overwatering symptoms on new plants include yellow tips and fronds; leaf drop; stem rot; pale new growth. Leaf tips on older foliage turn black. Underwatering symptoms are brown leaf tips; older fronds turn yellow, brown, then drop off; pale new growth with brown tips; canes lean out of the container.

MAINTENANCE TIPS: *Chamaedoreas* are easily stressed by improper watering and soluble salt build up. The foliage is sensitive and will develop spots or necrotic areas from improperly applied chemicals and fertilizers. Keep these palms healthy by keeping the foliage clean and pest free, the roots correctly watered and the nutrients in the growing media properly balanced. Refoliate thin plants by cutting canes down 1/4" above soil line.

PEST & DISEASE PROBLEMS: Spider mites, thrips, mealy bug, scale, soluble salt damage, stem and root rot (improper watering), leaf spot.

Chrysalidocarpus lutescens

COMMON NAME: Areca palm; butterfly palm; golden cane palm; yellow palm

FORM: Upright slim trunk with multiple arching feather shaped fronds

LIGHT RANGE: Medium to high light (100fc - 250fc+)

WATER REQUIREMENTS: In medium light water around stems; water entire root ball in high light. In medium light, allow media to dry down 1/3 of container; in higher light, 2" to 1/4 of container, depending on light intensity.

WATER STRESS SYMPTOMS: Underwatering symptoms start with brown tips, progressing to entire fronds turning yellow. Entire palm leans out of container. Small suckering growth dies back. Overwatering symptoms include yellowish tips on fronds. New growth turns yellow; roots develop rot.

MAINTENANCE TIPS: Suckering new growth will die off in light intensities under 100fc. *C. lutescens* is sensitive to temperatures below 50F. Excess soluble salts in media cause black spots and browning on foliage. Leach media regularly and add dolomitic lime to reduce fluoride damage. Low humidity causes brown tips on leaves.

PEST & DISEASE PROBLEMS: Spider mites, scale, thrips, mealy bug, stem and root rot, leaf spot.

Cissus rhombifolia, 'Ellen Danica'

COMMON NAME: Grape leaf ivy, 'Ellen Danica'

FORM: Bushy vine; hanging basket

LIGHT RANGE: Low to medium light (50fc - 250fc)

WATER REQUIREMENTS: Water new plants around base of stems. On older plants, thoroughly water entire root ball, then allow to dry sufficiently. In low light (50fc - 150fc), allow media to dry down 1/2 of container; in higher light conditions, allow media to dry down 1/3 of container.

WATER STRESS SYMPTOMS: Foliage on overwatered new plants turns black; foliage on established plants will turn a mottled yellow color. Over watered plants drop leaves and develop root and stem rot. Foliage on underwatered new plants turns bright yellow, then browns and falls off; foliage on established plants turns brown and falls off.

MAINTENANCE TIPS: *C. rhombifolia* is susceptible to powdery mildew, so water correctly and keep foliage dry. Pinch and prune regularly to keep plant from getting straggly and thin.

PEST & DISEASE PROBLEMS: Mealy bug, spider mites, powdery mildew.

Codiaeum variegatum

COMMON NAME: Croton

FORM: Bush

LIGHT RANGE: Medium to high light (150fc - 250+fc)

WATER REQUIREMENTS: Water new plants around base of stems; water established plants thoroughly, then allow to dry sufficiently. In medium light (150fc - 250fc), allow media to dry down 1/3 of container; in higher light conditions, allow media to dry down 2"-4" of container.

WATER STRESS SYMPTOMS: Overwatering symptoms include pale foliage, leaf drop, stem rot. Underwatering symptoms include brown tips, drooping foliage, leaf drop, withered stems.

MAINTENANCE TIPS: Crotons will drop leaves due to water stress, pest infestation, cold drafts and soluble salt build up. Allow plant to become rootbound to overcome overwatering problems. Crotons lose variegation in lower light conditions. Hand wash or spray foliage to keep clean and pest free.

PEST & DISEASE PROBLEMS: Spider mites, scale, mealy bug, thrips, stem rot, excess soluble salt damage.

©1992

Dieffenbachia species

COMMON NAME: Dumbcane, *Dieffenbachia*

FORM: Upright bushy

LIGHT RANGE: Medium to bright indirect light (80fc - 250+fc)

WATER REQUIREMENTS: In medium light water around stems only; in higher light water entire root ball. Allow plants in light intensities under 100fc to dry down 1/3 to 1/2 of container. Plants in higher light should dry down 1/4 to 1/3 of container.

WATER STRESS SYMPTOMS: Underwatering symptoms start with droopy foliage. Entire leaf turns bright yellow and stems lean out of container. Overwatering symptoms include yellowing foliage, pale new growth and dropping lower leaves. Plant develops stem and root rot.

MAINTENANCE TIPS: Low light conditions cause leaf drop of lower leaves, small new growth with thin, weak stems. *Dieffenbachias* are sensitive to cold drafts and temperatures below 60F. Wash foliage regularly to keep healthy and pest free. Rotate plant to promote even growth. Plant sap is toxic and may cause adverse dermal and oral reactions.

PEST & DISEASE PROBLEMS: Spider mites, thrips, mealybug, aphids, crown rot, stem rot, leaf spot.

Dracaena deremensis 'Janet Craig'

COMMON NAME: 'Janet Craig'

FORM: Upright bush

LIGHT RANGE: Low to medium light (50fc - 250fc)

WATER REQUIREMENTS: Water thoroughly, then allow media to dry. In low light (30fc - 100fc), allow media to dry down 1/2 of container; in medium light, 1/3 of container.

WATER STRESS SYMPTOMS: Overwatering symptoms start with yellowing leaf tips and progress to drooping foliage, pale new growth with necrotic tips and rotting roots and stems. Underwatering symptoms start with brown leaf tips and droopy foliage and progress to lower leaves turning completely yellow, stems leaning and collapsing and new growth looking pale and distorted.

MAINTENANCE TIPS: Hand wash leaves to keep clean. 'Janet Craigs' are sensitive to excessive fluoride and soluble salts and foliage will develop yellow blotches, brown tips and edges. Monitor pH levels, leach growing media and replace old growing media to delay symptoms. Apply epsom salts to counteract pale new growth due to magnesium deficiency.

PEST & DISEASE PROBLEMS: Spider mites, mealy bugs, thrips, stem and root rot, leaf blight, soluble salt build-up.

Dracaena deremensis 'Warneckii'

COMMON NAME: 'Warneckii;' striped dracaena

FORM: Upright bush; staggered cane

LIGHT RANGE: Low to medium light (50fc - 250fc)

WATER REQUIREMENTS: Water thoroughly, then allow media to dry. In low light (30fc - 100fc), allow media to dry down 1/2 of container; in medium light, 1/3 of container.

WATER STRESS SYMPTOMS: Overwatering and underwatering symptoms are similar to 'Janet Craig,' although 'Warneckiis' develop water stress symptoms quicker than 'Janet Craigs.'

MAINTENANCE TIPS: 'Warneckii's' foliage is brittle and develops mechanical damage easily. Hand wash leaves to keep clean. Like 'Janet Craigs,' 'Warneckiis' are sensitive to excessive fluoride and soluble salts in the growing media.

PEST & DISEASE PROBLEMS: Spider mites, mealy bugs, thrips, stem and root rot, leaf blight, soluble salt build-up.

©1992

Dracaena fragrans 'Massangeana'

COMMON NAME: Corn plant; cornstalk plant; mass cane

FORM: Staggered cane; bush; stump; wishbone; notched cane

LIGHT RANGE: Low to medium light (50fc - 250fc)

WATER REQUIREMENTS: Water new plants around canes only. Water entire root ball of older plants. In low light (30fc - 100fc), allow media to dry down 1/2 of container; in medium light, 1/3 of container.

WATER STRESS SYMPTOMS: Overwatering symptoms include yellowing tips, pale new growth with brown tips, root and stem rot. Underwatering symptoms includes drooping foliage with brown tips and curled margins. Older leaves turn brown. Canes are loose in pot and lean.

MAINTENANCE TIPS: New canes are under rooted and roots are damaged easily. Allow media to dry sufficiently before watering. Remove any flower spikes. Reduce soluble salt damage by using filtered water, leaching media, repotting plant, or replacing soil core samples with fresh soil. Keep foliage clean and pest free.

PEST & DISEASE PROBLEMS: Spider mites, mealy bugs, thrips, stem and root rots, soluble salt damage.

©1992

Dracaena marginata

COMMON NAME: *Marginata;* Madagascar dragon tree

FORM: Staggered upright; bush; character; standard

LIGHT RANGE: Low to medium (50fc - 250fc)

WATER REQUIREMENTS: Water thoroughly, then allow growing media to dry. In low light (35fc - 100fc), media should dry down 1/2 of container; in medium light, 1/3 of container. Water new plants around base of canes; water entire root ball of established plants with extensive root systems.

WATER STRESS SYMPTOMS: Overwatering symptoms include yellowing tips, root rot and pale new growth with brown tips. Canes will develop stem rot and feel mushy, with an unpleasant odor. Underwatering symptoms include droopy foliage and brown tips. Older leaves turn yellow, then brown and fall off; canes lean out of pot. New growth is pale and droopy.

MAINTENANCE TIPS: *Marginatas* are prone to root and stem rot, so allow growing media to dry out sufficiently between waterings. Plants can easily be shaped and pruned by cutting or breaking off foliage heads. Keep *marginatas* healthy by watering correctly and keeping foliage clean and pest free. Remove thick, upright leaves of new plants as they yellow; the new "indoor" leaves formed will be thinner, arching and better acclimated to the indoor environment.

PEST & DISEASE PROBLEMS: Spider mites, scale, mealy bug, stem and root rot, soluble salt damage.

Dracaena (Pleomele) reflexa

COMMON NAME: *Pleomele, reflexa*

FORM: Bush; multiple standard (tree form)

LIGHT RANGE: Medium to high light (150fc - 250+fc)

WATER REQUIREMENTS: Water thoroughly, then allow to dry sufficiently. In low light (50fc - 150fc), allow media to dry down 1/2 of container; in higher light conditions, allow media to dry down 1/3 of container.

©1992

WATER STRESS SYMPTOMS: Overwatering symptoms include foliage that turns yellowish and drops, mottled and pale new growth, root and stem rot. Underwatered foliage will turn bright yellow, then brown and drop. Stems shrivel and die.

MAINTENANCE TIPS: *Reflexas* are sensitive to water stress and are quick to drop leaves if watered improperly. Refoliate leggy, thin stems by pinching and pruning lateral branches.

PEST & DISEASE PROBLEMS: Spider mites, scale, mealy bug, leaf spot, die-back, root rot.

Epipremnum aureum

COMMON NAME: Pothos. Varieties include, 'Marble Queen', 'Golden', 'Jade'

FORM: Ground cover; hanging basket; upright totem pole

LIGHT RANGE: Low to medium light (50fc - 250fc)

WATER REQUIREMENTS: In underrooted new plants, water lightly around stems; water entire surface on older plants. In low light (30fc - 100fc), water lightly (do not soak Pothos) weekly or bi-weekly. A dribble of water on a regular basis is the rule for this shallow rooted plant (unlike most tropical plants). In higher light conditions, add more water, but never drench plant, or allow Pothos to sit in standing water.

WATER STRESS SYMPTOMS: Overwatering symptoms include rotting roots and mushy, black leaves on foliage closest to pot. Stems rot and pull easily out of container. Underwatering symptoms include leaves closest to pot begin to wilt, turn yellow then brown and die. Stems shrivel and wilt.

MAINTENANCE TIPS: Newly installed Pothos are underrooted and easily develop stem and root rots from improper watering. Older Pothos develop problems from compacted media high in soluble salts. Keep Pothos full by routinely pruning select vines back to 2" above soil line to promote new growth. Variegated varieties will lose color in low light conditions.

PEST & DISEASE PROBLEMS: Mealy bug, scale, spider mites, thrips, stem and root rot, leaf spot, soluble salt damage.

Ficus lyrata

COMMON NAME: Fiddle leaf fig, *lyrata*

FORM: Bush; standard (tree form)

LIGHT RANGE: Medium to high light (150fc - 250+fc)

WATER REQUIREMENTS: In lower light, water around base of stems; in higher light water thoroughly, then allow media to dry sufficiently. In medium light (150fc - 250fc), allow media to dry down 1/3 of container; in higher light conditions, allow media to dry down 2" to 1/4 of container.

WATER STRESS SYMPTOMS: Overwatering symptoms include central portion of leaf turns light green, foliage becomes mottled and yellowish, leaf drop, root rot. Underwatering symptoms include leaves turning brown and drooping, leaf drop, leaning stems, distorted new growth.

MAINTENANCE TIPS: Petioles are delicate and leaves will break off easily if damaged. *Lyratas* are sensitive to water stress and excess soluble salts and will develop blotches and mottled leaves. Pinch and prune branches to shape and refoliate plant. Hand wash leaves to keep clean.

PEST & DISEASE PROBLEMS: Scale, mealy bug, spider mites, excessive soluble salts, leaf spot, root rot.

©1992

Ficus species

COMMON NAME: Weeping fig, fig tree, *Ficus*. Varieties include *F. benjamina; F. retusa* 'Nitida'; *F. malcellandii* 'Alii'

FORM: Bush; standard (tree form); multiple standard; stump; braided; poodle cut; bonsai

LIGHT RANGE: Medium to high light (150fc - 250+fc)

WATER REQUIREMENTS: Water thoroughly and allow to dry sufficiently. Water under-rooted plants in lower light conditions around base of trunk. In medium light (100fc - 200fc), allow media to dry down 1/3 of container; in higher light conditions, allow media to dry down 2" to 1/4 of the container. Water requirements vary according to health of plant, environmental conditions and light levels.

WATER STRESS SYMPTOMS: Overwatering symptoms include green leaves dropping, pale new growth and root rot. Underwatering symptoms include yellowish brown leaves dropping and stems withering.

MAINTENANCE TIPS: Ficus species shed foliage due to water stress, changes in light conditions (acclimation), air pollution (mercury vapors) and cold drafts. Varieties such as *F. retusa* 'Nitida' and F. *malcellandii* 'Alii' are more tolerant than *F. benjamina*, and shed less foliage. Foliage develop yellow blotches due to excessive soluble salts. Prune branches to shape and refoliate thinning plants.

PEST & DISEASE PROBLEMS: Scale, mealy bugs, spider mites, excessive soluble salts, die-back, air pollution.

Flowering Plants

LIGHT RANGE: Low to high light (50fc - 250+fc)

WATER REQUIREMENTS: Water flowering plants thoroughly. In lower light conditions (50fc - 150fc), allow top 1/2" of media to dry; in higher light conditions, keep media evenly moist.

WATER STRESS SYMPTOMS: Overwatered plants drop flowers and yellowish leaves and will develop stem and root rot. Underwatered flowering plants will drop flowers, foliage turns brown and drops, stems wither and die.

MAINTENANCE TIPS: Most flowering plants used indoors are short term installations. To keep the flowers looking beautiful as long as possible, do not let media dry out. To regulate moisture levels, use subirrigation or add water-absorbing polymers. Raise humidity levels, if possible. Pick off spent blooms. Rotate plant weekly. Keep plant pest free.

PEST & DISEASE PROBLEMS: Aphids, thrips, scale, mealy bugs, whitefly, stem and root rot.

©1992

Howeia forsteriana

COMMON NAME: Kentia palm; sentry palm

FORM: Upright, arching palm

LIGHT RANGE: Low to medium light (50fc - 250fc)

WATER REQUIREMENTS: Water underrooted new plants lightly around base of stems; thoroughly water entire root ball of older plants with established roots. In low light (50fc - 100fc), allow plant to dry down 1/2 of container; in medium light, dry down 1/3 of container.

WATER STRESS SYMPTOMS: Overwatered kentias will initially develop yellow frond tips, then display yellowish speckling and turn brown. Roots develop root rot. Underwatering symptoms include brown leaf tips, droopy fronds and leaning stems. Smaller fronds turn yellow, then brown. The weight of the fronds can bend and damage stems, roots and may pull the entire plant out of the pot.

MAINTENANCE TIPS: Consider staking new palms to protect the shallow-rooted plant. Small stems will die back in lower light. Kentias are slow growers and will sustain only 4 to 5 fronds in low light; 10 fronds in higher light conditions.

PEST & DISEASE PROBLEMS: Spider mites, mealy bug, scale, thrips, root rot, soluble salt build up.

©1992

Neodypsis decaryi

COMMON NAME: Triangle palm

FORM: Arching upright palm with triangular shaped leaf base at top of trunk. Long feather shaped fronds grouped in three ranks on trunk.

LIGHT RANGE: Medium to bright indirect light (150fc - 250+fc)

WATER REQUIREMENT: Water entire root ball thoroughly. In medium light, allow media to dry down 1/3 of container; in higher light dry media down 3" to 1/4 of container, depending on light intensity.

WATER STRESS SYMPTOMS: Underwatering symptoms include brown tips starting on older foliage, progressing to entire fronds turning yellow, then brown and collapsing. New spears develop brown tips. Overwatering symptoms include brown or yellowish tips on fronds, progressing up until entire frond is discolored. Roots develop rot.

MAINTENANCE TIPS: Over fertilization leads to brown tips. Avoid placing in direct sun. Clean foliage regularly to keep healthy and pest-free.

PEST & DISEASE PROBLEMS: Spider mites, soft brown scale, mealybug. Crown and stem rot from overwatering.

©1992

Nephrolepsis exaltata 'Dallas'

COMMON NAME: Dallas fern

FORM: Compact bushy plant

LIGHT RANGE: Low to medium light (50fc - 250fc)

WATER REQUIREMENTS: Thoroughly water entire surface of media, then allow to dry sufficiently. In low light (50fc - 150fc), allow pot to dry slightly (2" below top of pot); in higher light, keep moist.

WATER STRESS SYMPTOMS: Overwatering symptoms include blackened, broken fronds. Fronds may be pale green and limp. Plant develops rhizome and root rot. Underwatering symptoms start as pale green fronds. Petioles will bend and fronds will turn brown and fall off.

MAINTENANCE TIPS: Groom off all brown foliage. Cut bent and broken fronds back to soil line. *N. exaltata* has an extensive root system, so be sure entire root ball is moistened when watering. Gradual yellowing and a general decline may indicate inadequate lighting, overwatering or low humidity. Change environmental conditions to improve overall health.

PEST & DISEASE PROBLEMS: Scale, mealy bug, aphids, spider mites, thrips, rhizome and root rot.

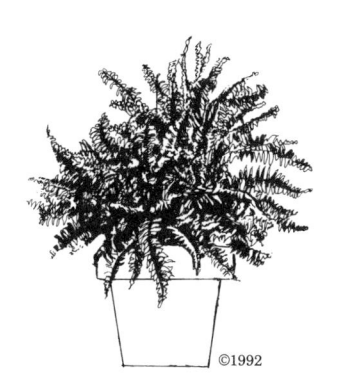

Phoenix roebelenii

COMMON NAME: Miniature date palm, pygmy date palm, *Phoenix* palm

FORM: Compact arching palm

LIGHT RANGE: Medium to high light (150fc - 250+fc)

WATER REQUIREMENTS: Thoroughly water entire root ball, then allow to dry sufficiently. In medium light (100fc - 250fc), allow media to dry down 1/3 of container; in higher light conditions, allow to dry down 3" to 1/3 of container.

WATER STRESS SYMPTOMS: Overwatering symptoms start with yellowing foliage and then progress to entire fronds that collapse and wilt. Roots develop rot and entire plant declines rapidly. Underwatering symptoms start with brown tips that progress to entire fronds turning brown and collapsing. The dense root system makes it difficult for water to penetrate into the center of the root ball, so water dry media carefully.

MAINTENANCE TIPS: *Phoenix* palms have extensive fleshy root systems that store water. Plant will decline rapidly if overwatered in low light conditions. Low humidity causes brown tips on fronds. Hand wash or spray fronds to keep clean. Remove lower older fronds as they decline. *Phoenix* palms have only one single point of growth per trunk. Do not damage the new growth of the palm or the plant will decline and die. Water dry media in stages to moisten entire rootball.

PEST & DISEASE PROBLEMS: Spider mites, scale, mealy bug, thrips, crown and root rot.

Polyscias balfouriana

COMMON NAME: Balfour aralia

FORM: Bush; multiple stem

LIGHT RANGE: Medium to high light (150fc - 250+fc)

WATER REQUIREMENTS: In medium light, water around base of stems, then allow media to dry down 1/2 of container. In high light conditions (250+fc), water thoroughly and allow media to dry down 1/3 of container.

WATER STRESS SYMPTOMS: Overwatering symptoms include yellowish foliage, leaf drop, stem and root rot. Underwatering shows up as withered stems, brown leaves, drooping foliage and leaf drop.

MAINTENANCE TIPS: Balfours are sensitive plants and will drop foliage due to water stress, air pollution (ethylene gas), low humidity, or cold temperatures. Leaves develop brown tips due to low humidity. Remove foliage by gently raking fingers through foliage clumps each week. Spray foliage to keep clean and pest free. Pinch and prune branches to shape and refoliate plant.

PEST & DISEASE PROBLEMS: Spider mites, mealy bug, scale.

©1992

Ravenea rivularis

COMMON NAME: Majesty palm

FORM: Upright palm with arching fronds

LIGHT RANGE: Medium to high light (150fc - 250+fc)

WATER REQUIREMENTS: *R. rivularis* has an extensive root system and entire root ball needs to be watered thoroughly. In medium light (150fc - 250fc), allow media to dry down 1/4 of container; in high light (250fc+) dry media down only 2-3".

WATER STRESS SYMPTOMS: Underwatering symptoms include brown tips on fronds, starting first on older foliage. If dryness persists, entire fronds turn bright yellow. Overwatering symptoms include yellowish frond tips. Yellowing extends up frond until entire frond is discolored. Roots develop rot.

MAINTENANCE TIPS: Wash fronds regularly to keep palm healthy. Do not damage the terminal growth point in center of trunk. Prune off older fronds that discolor with age and die. Monitor growing media for pH and soluble salt content.

PEST & DISEASE PROBLEMS Soft brown scale, spider mites, mealybug. Crown or root rot from overwatering.

Rhapis excelsa

COMMON NAME: Lady palm; *Rhapis* palm

FORM: Upright bush; tree form

LIGHT RANGE: Low to medium light (50fc - 250fc)

WATER REQUIREMENTS: Thoroughly water entire root ball, then allow to dry sufficiently. In low light (50fc - 100fc), allow to dry down 1/2 of container; in medium light, 1/3/ of container.

WATER STRESS SYMPTOMS: Overwatering symptoms include yellowing leaf tips and droopy foliage. Roots develop rot. Underwatering symptoms include yellowish fronds with brown leaf tips, collapsed, drooping leaves and leaning trunks. Roots are woody as opposed to fleshy and dry out quicker than other palms.

MAINTENANCE TIPS: *Rhapis* palms like high humidity and will develop brown tips in low humidity. Trim brown edges with pinking shears to simulate normal foliage. Refoliate thinning plants by cutting leggy trunks to 1" above soil line and allowing suckering growth to sprout up. *Rhapis* are sensitive to excessive fluoride and soluble salts in growing media and will develop yellowing blotches and brown tips under these conditions.

PEST & DISEASE PROBLEMS: Mealy bug, spider mites, scale, thrips, soluble salt build up.

©1992

Sansevieria trifasciata

COMMON NAME: Snake plant; Mother-in-law's tongue; *Sansevieria*

FORM: Upright clump

LIGHT RANGE: Low to medium light (50fc - 250fc)

WATER REQUIREMENTS: Water thoroughly, then allow to dry out sufficiently. In low light (20fc - 100fc), allow to dry down 3/4 of pot; in medium light, 1/2 to 3/4 of container.

WATER STRESS SYMPTOMS: Symptoms of overwatering begin with yellowish tips on leaf blades. Blades turn mushy and smelly from stem rot of the rhizomes (underground stems). Roots develop rot. Underwatering symptoms include brown tips, shrivelled roots and leaf blades, drooping foliage.

MAINTENANCE TIPS: *Sansevierias* have thick rhizomes that store water for long periods of time. Growing media should be dried sufficiently and leaf blades should feel spongy to the touch before adding additional water. Do not damage the tip of the leaf as the blade will not grow if terminal growth point is broken or cut.

PEST & DISEASE PROBLEMS: Scale, mealy bug, nematodes, leaf and root rot.

©1992

Spathiphyllum species

COMMON NAME: Spaths; peace lily. Varieties include 'Lynese'; 'Supreme'; 'Mauna Loa Supreme'; Sensation'; 'Starlight'; 'Petite'

FORM: Upright clump

LIGHT RANGE: Low to medium light (50fc - 250fc)

WATER REQUIREMENTS: Water thoroughly, then allow media to dry sufficiently. In low light (40fc - 100fc), allow growing media to dry down 1/3 of container; in medium light, dry down 1/4 to 1/3 of pot. Water requirements will fluctuate due to environmental conditions, seasonal changes, and overall health of the plant.

WATER STRESS SYMPTOMS: Overwatering symptoms include yellowing tips, leaf blades wilted and curled, root rot and eventual collapse of plant. Underwatering symptoms start with leaf blades looking dull and droopy, then progress to entire leaves wilting and petioles collapsing; flower spathes wilt and turn brown; brown leaf tips; smaller, newer leaves turn yellowish and die.

MAINTENANCE TIPS: White "flowers", or spathe are produced in higher light and when plant is root bound. Remove spadix (floral spike enclosed in spathe) from spathe to prolong flowering and to prevent pollen from shedding. Keep plant healthy by keeping foliage clean and pest free and by maintaining the proper moisture levels in the medium.

PEST & DISEASE PROBLEMS: Mealybugs, spider mites, scale, thrips, whitefly, root rot, soluble salt damage.

Strelitzia nicolai

COMMON NAME: White bird of paradise

FORM: Upright arching palm

LIGHT RANGE: High light (250+fc)

WATER REQUIREMENTS: Water thoroughly, then allow to dry sufficiently. Allow media to dry down 4" to 1/4 of container, depending on light and temperature conditions.

WATER STRESS SYMPTOMS: Overwatered plants exhibit yellowish mottled foliage that turns brown. Underwatering symptoms include droopy fronds with brown tips and edges. Entire foliage turns brown and curls.

MAINTENANCE TIPS: Low humidity causes brown tips and new fronds have difficulty opening. To produce flowers, plants need to be mature, healthy specimens growing in high light conditions. Hand wash foliage to keep clean.

PEST & DISEASE PROBLEMS: Mealy bug, spider mites.

©1992

Glossary of Terms

Abiotic diseases: (see noninfectious diseases)

Acclimatization: the process by which a plant adapts to its new environment.

Axillary buds: latent dormant buds found at each node.

Auxins: hormones that regulate various plant functions.

Bacteria: single-celled, non spore forming microscopic organisms. They usually enter the host plant through wounds or natural openings.

Biological controls: a pest control strategy that uses living organisms to control another less desirable living organism.

Biotic diseases: (see infectious diseases)

Branch bark collar: swelling at the base of a branch that contains natural antibodies that help ward of disease pathogens.

Capillary matting: super absorbing cotton wicking material used in some subirrigation systems.

Chemical controls: pesticides and least toxic chemicals such as rubbing alcohol and phosphate-free soap used to control pests.

Cultural/mechanical control: techniques used to change the plant's physical environment, the condition of the host plant or the behavior of the pest in order to prevent or suppress the pest.

Fertilizers: a combination of minerals needed by plant to produce carbohydrates during photosynthesis.

Flowers: the plant's reproductive organs.

Fungi: minute organisms lacking chlorophyll. Fungi produce spores which can spread easily from plant to plant. These living pathogens cause diseases such as leaf spots, stem and root rots, blights and powdery mildew.

Growing media: a combination of media particles, water and pore spaces. The media used by most tropical plants contain no soil (referred to as a soilless media), and is a combination of organic matter such as peat moss and bark mixed with inorganic materials like perlite, vermiculite, or styrofoam pellets.

Honeydew: a clear sticky residue exuded by insects.

Infectious diseases: a disease caused by a living pathogen such as a fungus, bacteria or virus.

Integrated Pest Management: a method of pest control that combines cultural, mechanical, biological and least toxic chemical solutions.

Internode: space between nodes on a stem.

IPM: (see integrated pest management)

Light duration: refers to the total number of hours of light a plant receives in a day (also called photoperiod).

Light Intensity: refers to the brightness of light. It is measured in "footcandles" (the amount of light that one 'international candle' will emit over one square of surface when the candle is one foot away).

Light Quality: refers to the different wave lengths of colors that make up the visible (white) light.

Leaves: produce food for the plant through process of photosynthesis. The leaf is composed of the blade and petiole. Leaves may be classified as simple (with one blade), or compound (the blade composed of many leaflets).

Macro nutrients: major nutrients that plants need for growth. They include carbon, hydrogen, oxygen, nitrogen, phosphorus, potassium, calcium, magnesium and sulfur. Called macro nutrients because the plant uses them in large amounts.

Mechanical controls: (see cultural/mechanical control)

Micro nutrients: micro or trace elements needed in small amounts for plant growth. The micro nutrients include iron, zinc, boron, copper, manganese, molybdenum and chlorine.

Node: the point where a leaf is attached to a stem.

Noninfectious diseases: a disease that develops from abiotic or non living disease agents. Noninfectious diseases can develop due to incorrect environmental conditions, poor maintenance practices, or aging media.

Pathogen: a disease-producing organism.

pH: the measure of relative acidity of the growing media.

Permanent wilting point (PWP): the point at which vascular cells collapse due to wilting. The plant will not recover at this point.

Phloem: vascular cells that transport food and auxins downward from the foliage.

Photosynthesis: the process by which plants use water, minerals and carbon dioxide and, in the presence of sunlight, produce carbohydrates (plant food).

Phytotoxic reactions: an adverse reaction to a chemical or pesticide.

Pinching plants: a technique that involves removing the growing tip (apex) of a plant to promote lateral branching.

Pore spaces: empty areas or holes in growing media. The pore spaces are filled with either air or moisture; both of which are needed by the roots.

Pruning: a technique that involves removing stems and branches of a plant. This is done to force new growth, control the shape of the plant or to control an infection or infestation.

Relative humidity: refers to the amount of moisture held in the air.

Respiration: the opposite of photosynthesis; the process by which a plant breaks down stored carbohydrates for energy.

Roots: absorb nutrients and moisture for the plant through root hairs at tip of roots. Help anchor plant in container and help purify the air by filtering toxic air through media during respiration.

Sessile leaves: leaves without a petiole; leaf blade is attached directly to the stem (example: Dracaena marginata).

Soluble salts: a build up of salts from fertilizers, poor quality water or decomposing organic matter in the media.

Sooty mold: a black, powdery fungal disease that develops on the honeydew exuded from insects.

Subirrigation: subirrigation or self-watering containers are systems that supply moisture to a plant on a regular basis. A reservoir of water is located at the bottom of the container. Plants draw up moisture as they need it.

Stems: supports plant, stores excess carbohydrates and transports water, minerals, growth hormones and food through plant. Leaves are attached to stem at a node.

Stomates: microscopic opening on the undersides of leaves. Stomates exchange gases and cool the leaf surface by transpiring water vapor.

Top watering: adding water to the top of the container.

Translocation: movement of water and minerals through the plant.

Transpiration: the process by which a plant cools its leaf surface. Water vapor is transpired through the stomates to lower the temperature levels.

Vector: an insect or other organism transmitting germs or other agents of disease.

Viruses: microscopic pathogens, consisting of a single strand of DNA and a protein coating. They can enter a host plant through injuries or insect damage.

Xylem: Vascular cells that transport water and minerals up from the roots.

Index

Abiotic disease, 43, 44, 45
Acclimatization, 5
Aglaonema, 54
Air pollution, 23
Aphids, 31
Areca palm, 60
Auxins, 4, 13
Axillary bud, 3, 13, 15
Bacteria, 40
Balfour aralia, 77
Bamboo palm, 59
Beaucarnea recurvata, 55
Biological controls, 49, 50, 51
Bird of paradise, 82
Blight, 37, 39
Brassaia actinophylla, 56
Cactaceae family, 57
Caryota mitis, 58
Cation exchange capacity, 27
Chamaedorea species, 59
Chlorophyll, 4, 5, 37
Chrysalidocarpus lutescens, 60
Cissus rhombifolia, 61
Codiaeum variegatum, 62
Croton, 62
Dallas fern, 75
Date palm, 76
Dieffenbachia species, 63
Disease, 9, 15, 22, 35, 37, 39, 40, 43, 44, 45, 47
Dracaena, 64, 65, 66, 67, 68
Epipremnum aureum, 69
Feather dusters, 11
Fertilizers, 11, 27, 28, 29, 31, 32, 33, 43
Ficus lyrata, 70
Ficus species, 71
Fishtail palm, 58
Flowers, 3, 17, 72
Foot candles, 21
Fungi, 9, 37
Fungus gnats, 31
Grape leaf ivy, 61
Grooming plants, 11, 12, 43, 49
Growing media, 3, 7, 8, 9, 25, 29, 32, 40, 43
Honeydew, 31, 32, 33, 35, 45
Howeia forsteriana, 73
Horticultural oil, 31, 32, 33, 35
Humidity, 4, 5, 17, 21, 22, 23, 35, 40, 43, 49
Infectious diseases, 37, 39, 40
Insecticidal soap, 11, 31, 32, 33, 35, 49, 50
Integrated pest management, 31, 32, 33, 35, 49, 50, 51
Internode, 3
Janet Craig, 64
Kentia, 73
Leaves, 3, 5, 7, 9, 11, 12, 13, 21, 23, 27, 39, 49
Light, 3, 5, 7, 17, 21, 22, 27, 28, 35, 43, 49
Majesty palm, 78
Marginata, 67
Massangeana cane, 66
Molds, 9
Neodypsis decaryi, 74
Nephrolepis exaltata, 75
Node, 3
Noninfectious disease, 43, 44, 45, 49
Nutrients, 3, 4, 5, 7, 25, 27, 28, 29, 43, 49
Overwatering, 8, 9, 43, 49
Pathogen, 37
Perlite, 25
Permanent wilting point, 9
Pest infestations, 22, 31, 32, 33, 35, 40, 49, 50
Pesticides, 31, 32, 33, 35, 49, 50, 51
Petiole, 3, 9
pH, 25, 28, 29, 43
Phloem, 4
Phoenix roebelenii, 76
Photoperiod, 21, 43
Photosynthesis, 3, 4, 7, 23, 31, 43
Phytotoxic reactions, 11, 44
Pinching plants, 12, 13, 49
Polyscias balfouriana, 77
Ponytail palm, 55
Pore space, 3, 7, 8, 25
Pothos, 69
Powdery Mildew, 31, 32, 35, 37, 39
Pruning plants, 12, 15, 17, 22, 27, 31, 32, 35, 40, 43, 49
Ravenea rivularis, 78
Reflexa, 68
Respiration, 3, 4, 23, 25
Rhapis excelsa, 79
Roots, 3, 4, 7, 9, 22, 23, 25, 27, 31, 32, 43
Sansevieria trifasciata, 80
Scale, armored, 32, 33
Scale, soft, 32, 33

86 \ INDEX

Schefflera arboricola, 56
Sessile leaves, 3
Silver Queen, 54
Snake plant, 80
Soap, 11, 27, 31, 32, 33, 35, 49, 50
Soluble salts, 8, 25, 27, 28, 29, 43
Spathiphyllum species, 81
Sphagnum peat moss, 25, 27
Spider mites, 22, 33, 35, 45
Spore, 37
Stem, 3, 9, 39
Stomates, 3, 4
Strelitzia nicolai, 82
Subirrigation, 8, 17, 27, 29
Temperatures, 4, 15, 17, 21, 22, 43, 45, 49

Thrips, 35
Translocation, 3, 4, 7
Transpiration, 4
Triangle palm, 74
Trimming plants, 12, 43, 49
Underwatering, 7, 9, 17, 43
Vermiculite, 25
Viruses, 40
Warneckii, 65
Watering, 3, 7, 8, 17, 22, 23, 25, 27, 29, 37, 40, 43, 49
Water of Guttation, 5
Whitefly, 35
Wilt, 5, 7, 9, 17, 21, 22, 28, 43
Xylem, 4

Index to "Tips"

Acclimating plants, 5
Are you a 'vector'?, 41
Become a plant detective, 47
Caring for flowering plants, 17
Cleaning the tough stuff, 11
Controlling soluble salts, 29
Diagnosing abiotic diseases (chart), 44
Disease-free tools, 39
Drying out saturated media, 8
First aid for wilted plants, 5
Healing your plant, 43
Is it time to water?, 8

Living with available light, 22
Pinching keeps plants bushy, 13
Plant grooming list, 12
Prevent diseases on your plants, 37
Pruning to force new growth, 15
Reviving a wilted plant, 9
Stabilizing humidity levels, 23
The keys to integrated pest management, 51
Using beneficial organisms, 50
When NOT to fertilize, 28
Your plant's food production, 27

About the Authors

Susan McCollum and Teena Risley have over 25 years of experience in interior landscaping. They have cared for tropicals and flowering plants in commercial spaces and have trained staff in plant care techniques.

Susan McCollum, a Certified Interior Landscape Professional, served as vice president for a Virginia interior and exterior landscaping firm and garden center. She received Environmental Improvement Awards for her work with interior landscapes. Ms. McCollum is a graduate of Ohio University with degrees in education and journalism.

Teena Risley graduated from the University of Vermont with a degree in plant and soil science. She has devoted her entire career to the field of interiorscaping, working as a horticultural technician, supervisor and trainer. Most recently, she owned an interiorscape company and served as a training consultant for local interiorscape companies.

McCollum, Risley & Associates was established in 1992 to promote professionalism in the interiorscape industry through training and education. Ms. McCollum and Ms. Risley publish *Tropical Plant Technician,* a monthly newsletter for horticultural technicians. They speak at industry related conferences and training seminars, and serve as industry consultants. In an effort to share their plant care tips with the public, Ms. McCollum and Ms. Risley have hosted educational television shows about indoor gardening and taught horticulture classes in local adult education programs.